THE TOM SANFORD STORY

wounded healer

from a **childhood** of abuse
to a ministry of
healing

Tom Sanford
with Kay D. Rizzo

D0017500

Pacific Press® Publishing Association
Nampa, Idaho
Oshawa, Ontario, Canada
www.pacificpress.com

Design by Michelle C. Petz
Cover photo by John LeMay

Copyright © 2005 by
Pacific Press® Publishing Association
Printed in the United States of America
All rights reserved

Some names in *Wounded Healer* have been changed to protect indi-
viduals' identities.

Additional copies of this book are available by calling toll-free
1-800-765-6955 or by visiting www.adventistbookcenter.com

Library of Congress Cataloging-in-Publication Data

Sanford, Tom, 1943–
Wounded healer: from a childhood of abuse to a ministry of healing:
the Tom Sanford story/Tom Sanford and Kay D. Rizzo.
p. cm.
ISBN: 0-8163-2108-6
ISBN 13: 9780816321087
1. Sanford, Tom, 1943– 2. Project Patch (Youth facility) 3. Problem
youth—Services for—Idaho. 4. Social work with youth—Idaho.
5. Adult child abuse victims—Biography. I. Rizzo, Kay D., 1943–
II. Title.

HV1435.I2S36 2006
362.74'8'0979674—dc22   2005050897

05 06 07 08 09 · 5 4 3 2 1

dedication

To my wife, Bonnie, who has stood beside me through the thick and thin of life and has been the "mother" to many children and teenagers. Her tireless persistence that something needed to be done for hurting children became the backbone for Project PATCH.

acknowledgments

We have too little space to express our appreciation to myriads of people who have made Project PATCH possible and who have helped create a program that excels in providing a caring and Christian program for hundreds of young people over the years. Fearing the possibility of forgetting someone, I will acknowledge people by categories.

Donors: Without our donors we could not have accomplished what we have. We certainly would not have been able to offer young people the opportunity to turn their lives around and face adulthood with a focus where previously there was none. Some donors have made financial sacrifices to provide help for hurting children. Others have donated material, vehicles, equipment, airplanes, and property to make PATCH the fine residential treatment program that it is.

Board of trustees: The first board members exhibited much faith and vision when they met to discuss and plan the future of an unfunded innovative project. The subsequent board members accepted the challenge of dealing with growth and the occasional crises that took place as PATCH faced some surprising obstacles. All board members deserve gratitude for guiding PATCH as it developed from an idea into a thriving facility.

Staff: The long-term commitment of the PATCH staff provides consistency that at-risk children need. At PATCH the length of employment far exceeds the average work expectancy of an employee in the child-treatment field. Also inspiring is the way God brought special talents to our staff at just the time we needed their expertise, beginning with the construction stages and through the present time. As the needs at PATCH changed, staff was available to meet the needs.

Maranatha: Without the Maranatha volunteers who have come to every construction project at the ranch—thirteen projects since 1991—the physical plant would have cost more and been built more slowly. Every building at the ranch has been built, remodeled, or in some way been touched by these volunteers, who have made PATCH a better and safer place for young people to live.

Volunteers: In addition to people from Marantha volunteers, there have been those who have come, from the beginning, to help with building projects and with mentoring the young people.

To our Lord and Savior, Jesus Christ: We thank You for loving every one of us so much that You died for us. We thank You for instilling in us the desire to see in others the best and not the worst. We thank You for reminding us that there is no pit so deep and no place so far away that You are not willing to come find us and bring us back to You. These young people are Yours—we are only here as Your ambassadors, sheepherders to lead the lambs to You.

contents

introduction

It came as a shock to both Tom and me to realize that we really didn't know ourselves until after we got married. The way our parents' speech and actions popped up out of nowhere into Tom and my interactions was unnerving. We found ourselves repeating the behavioral patterns we had most hated from our childhoods.

Tom and I came from similar backgrounds. Both of us were raised in a male-dominated household in which the father used anger to control his family. Our fathers were "king" babies—the youngest child following five or six siblings. Both fathers grew up demanding and getting what they wanted, when they wanted it. Both men married good women who bore them several children, thus exempting the men from any military service. Neither father could relate to other males and, as a result, were abusive to male family members. Tom was the scapegoat for his family. He smiled too much, which irritated his father. When anything went wrong, Tom suffered for it.

Both fathers were chameleons—Dr. Jekyll and Mr. Hyde—very nice in public and very selfish and vindictive at home. Both men struggled to provide food and shelter for their families. As a result, they moved their families from place to place. My family moved twenty-two times before I entered high school.

So naturally, by the similarities of our backgrounds, Tom and I found ourselves magnetically drawn to one another. Financially broke, in college, in love, and having no home or family to turn to for guidance, we naively bumbled into the marriage contract. The greatest advantage we had going for us was God. He loved us unconditionally, and we both loved Him. Independent of each other, we had dedicated our lives to His service—I as a teacher, and Tom as a minister.

As I contemplated marriage, I was certain I could make a peaceful, secure, and happy home for myself and my husband-to-be. We would nurture each other. And, of course, because we both loved God, a kind, gentle spirit would radiate throughout our home.

Unfortunately, day-by-day living is seldom so tidy. The past all too easily bullies itself into the present. Verbal assaults and the inability to communicate in a loving and mature manner were our reality. The ability to love and nurture were foreign to both of us. We couldn't pull it off.

Lest you think this is a tragic tale concocted in someone's imagination, I can assure you that it is all too true. I was not touched, hugged, or told I was loved by either of my parents until years later, when I forced my mother to tell me by phone that she loved me. Her biological mother had died when she was seven, and she had been raised by the proverbial "wicked stepmother." While Tom's mother told him she loved him, she couldn't or wouldn't protect him from his abusive father.

Little things from one's past take major importance in shaping the present. For example, today I can look back and understand why I would never agree with Tom to live in a home that had more than one level. Dodging a glass ashtray my father heaved at my head in anger is one of the many flashbacks I still have from childhood. I remember running as fast as my six-year-old legs could carry me up the stairs and hiding under a rollaway bed in which my two oldest sisters slept. (My other sister and I slept on the floor.) There I curled into a fetal ball and hardly dared breathe while my father searched for me. I thought I was safe from my father's fury until the bed moved and I felt the sharp metal belt buckle lashing my legs. Such events were typical.

And now, thirty-eight years later, I can say that only a loving God, through His Son's blood and the guidance of the Holy Spirit, could mend our broken lives. Together, Tom and I nurtured our own wounded childhood through the joys and experiences of being parents to our children, Kelly and Craig. Yet somewhere, deep down inside, we longed to reach out to other hurting young people, to give others what we'd missed. We could relate to their experiences; we could believe their stories. Our past experiences could contribute to their hope for the future.

—Bonnie Sanford

nightmares
into dreams

The narrow trail up the rocky slope beckoned me, as it always did whenever the demons of childhood bombarded my subconscious. I hiked the trail with ease until I reached the crest of the gorge, where I paused to inhale the rich aromas of evergreens and moist earth. Looking north, a ribbon of gray meandered from east to west—the Columbia River. Beyond the river, a thick belt of fir trees announced the Washington State border.

I wheeled about, eager to continue my hike on the trail through thick undergrowth. Instead, I found myself facing an open field of long grasses and wild flowers, burnt by summer's scorching sun. In the middle of the field stood a giant tree unlike those indigenous to western Oregon. A sense of dread washed over me and settled in the pit of my stomach. I recognized the hated maple tree and realized that I was no longer in Oregon, but twenty-eight hundred miles east, in Pennsylvania.

My feet ignored my brain's signals to flee, and I stood paralyzed for several seconds, uncertain of where I was or how I'd gotten there. A child's wail startled me. Thinking someone must be hurt or lost, I rushed toward the cry. I was within fifty yards of the gnarled old tree before I saw the chain, wrapped around the tree trunk and hooked to a dog collar. The dog collar circled the neck of a sobbing child who couldn't have been more than two years old.

Shocked that anyone would do such a thing to a toddler, I sprinted across the grass to his aid. When I was within fifteen feet of the boy, a man stepped out from behind the tree. He waved a stick over his head and screamed at the child.

"You are worthless! A dummy! A pantywaist! I hate your guts!" His rough, gravelly voice boomed across the field.

"Stop! Stop!" I knew that I had to save the child from a certain beating.

The man whipped about to face me, the menacing stick high over his head. As he focused his gaze on me, he grew in stature until he loomed fifteen feet or more above my head. "Who are you?"

"Stop!" Though I shouted as loud as I could, my words were but a whimper.

"Who do you think you are?" The man angled around me, ready to strike. "You stupid, worthless, piece of . . ." As he swung his weapon toward my head, I threw my hands up to protect myself.

"No-o-o-o-o!" I tried to cry out. I tried to run, but my legs spun helplessly in place, like automobile tires on ice. No, this can't be real! I willed myself awake.

The field, the tree, and the man disappeared; and I found myself in a warm and familiar cocoon of darkness. In the soft moonlight coming in through our bedroom window, I could make out the form of my wife, Bonnie. I exhaled sharply.

"Honey, are you OK?" Her voice was fuzzy from sleep. "Was it a dream again?"

"Yeah!" I couldn't breathe. Cold sweat beaded my forehead. Tears ran down my face, saturating my pillowcase.

"Well, you surely scared me!" She laughed. "I thought it was the beginning of the apocalypse!"

I gave a nervous chuckle. Bonnie could always make me laugh, in spite of myself. "I'm sorry I wakened you."

She slipped under my rigid arm and rested her head on my chest. "It's OK. If anyone understands, I do."

Bonnie had also come from what is commonly called a "dysfunctional" family. Over the years we'd seen one another through uncountable bouts of tears, agonizing nightmares, and numerous journeys down venomous memory lanes.

After a few minutes, I disentangled myself from her arms and sat up, threw back the covers, and slid my legs over the edge of the bed. "I-I-I need a drink of water. I need to be alone."

"I love you." Bonnie rolled over to go back to sleep.

The pattern was always the same. It would begin with a horrendous nightmare. Sometimes I would be trapped in an old barn with a lion or bear and be unable to locate the barn door. Sometimes I'd find the door, only to realize it wouldn't budge. I would awaken to find myself in a cold sweat. I would then slip away to my study to give the artesian well of terror I suppressed deep inside of me time to subside. I hated the fact that my father could still reach out and affect my life after all these years.

The source of my nightmare came from a very real occurrence in my life. I remember being lashed to a tree with a chain and a dog collar fastened around my neck. Somehow I'd wandered off, and my father accused me of running away. To teach me a lesson, he let the dog go and chained me to the tree trunk. I was two. It was the first time I remember my father telling me that he hated my "guts." I didn't know what "guts" were, but I knew it had to be pretty bad because my father looked so angry.

I grew up being afraid of my dad. I was so scared of him I would do anything to please him. But try as I might, I couldn't make him happy with me. Whenever something broke down on the farm and I happened to be close by, he whipped, beat, or kicked me. Whenever a tractor wouldn't start, I was to blame. Whenever I smiled or looked like I might smile, he'd slap or kick me and tell me, "Wipe that smile off your face, Boy, or I'll wipe it off for you!"

I wasn't the only one to suffer at his hand. Our pets felt his rage as well. One day he came in from the barn and found our tabby housecat licking butter from an uncovered butter dish on the kitchen table. Furious, he grabbed the animal by the neck, stormed outside, and hurled it against a tree trunk. Cats are supposed to have nine lives, but this one didn't have a chance to live two.

When I was seven, we had a golden-brown mutt we named Tippie. At night, Tippie loved to sleep at the foot of my bed and keep my feet warm. I could depend on Tippie to be there for me. I would bury my face in his fur whenever I needed a friend. One day my father took Tippie over the hill and shot him for reasons my young mind couldn't understand. That night my faithful friend didn't return to the house; he didn't hop up on the foot of my bed. I cried myself to sleep.

In the morning while I was milking the cows, Tippie appeared at the barn door, his fur matted with blood. "Tippie! You're alive!" I didn't dare speak above a whisper. The dog limped over to me and lay down beside me. I hugged him, matted fur and all. The look of pain and confusion in his soulful, brown eyes broke my young heart. Tears welled up in my eyes and then ran down my cheeks. I could barely see clearly enough to finish milking the cow. I had to do something to help my friend. Frantically, I glanced about the barn. Where could I hide him? Where could I keep Tippie safe from my dad? In the hay loft? In the tool shed? I thought about all the possibilities. But before I could formulate a plan, my father strode into the barn..

"What's that mutt doing here? I thought I finished him off yesterday!" Grabbing Tippie, he dragged the dog out the door. On his way he grabbed the gun he always kept loaded in the barn. "Keep milking!"

"No, Dad, please don't!" My cries fell on deaf ears. Time stood still as I buried my head in the flank of the cow I was milking. I winced as I heard the single rifle shot. I never saw my friend again.

Before I was born, my grandparents had purchased a hundred-acre farm and given it to my father. Grandpa also gave us a team of horses, along with a couple of old tractors. In the summer it was my job to hitch the horses to the one-row cultivator and cultivate the corn. My father refused to let me drive the tractors. "You're too much of a sissy to drive heavy machinery. Boy, you will never amount to anything no matter how long you live!" During the day Dad worked at another job while the four of us boys did the farming and baby-sat our little sister, Diana.

My grandparents were my only refuge. They would play with me, laugh with me, and hug me—gentle, loving treatment I never received at home. At their house no one called me dummy, stupid, worthless, sissy, pantywaist, ugly, and other names too crude to repeat.

I was thirteen when my father sold the farm, packed up the family, and moved us to Wisconsin, where he purchased a 320-acre farm, along with a collection of new machinery. It was a strange place. Every building on the farm was made of old boxcars—the barns, the garage, the shed, even the house. How my mother managed to make the house homey, I'll never know. We hadn't lived there a year when a stranger came by one day and hauled off the tractor and farm machinery. He left the horses, the manure wagon, and the cultivator. The next day another individual came for the cows. All we had left was the land and the rusty boxcars. Without explanation, we loaded our household goods onto an old International truck and moved to another farm my father had rented. We lived in an old farmhouse with no indoor plumbing until a stranger repossessed the new cows my father had purchased.

Having lost everything to the bank, my father took a job managing a farm for someone else. With dad home all day, the beatings got worse and more frequent. One day he hit me so hard that he knocked me unconscious. His outbursts left visible marks on me too. At school the other children called me "fat lips and red eyes." By the age of fifteen, I believed that it was only a matter of time before my father would kill me like he had Tippie and the family cat. I never thought I'd reach adulthood. And if I did, I wouldn't amount to anything anyway. He'd convinced me I was useless and the beatings were all my fault.

I was afraid to live, afraid of what was going to happen next. I was also afraid to die. At night I would lie awake and wonder how long it would hurt before I didn't know anything more. Only my fear that the pain of dying was worse than the pain I'd already experienced kept me alive.

After a while we moved to yet another dairy farm that my father was hired to manage. Every morning my brothers and I helped milk fifty cows before we left for school. It was my job to feed the cows and to keep their water cups clean. One morning while I was cleaning Maddy's (all the cows had names) cup, the water wouldn't stop running. Frantic, I desperately tried to turn it off, but everything was getting soaked. I rushed to where my father was milking. "Dad, Maddy's water cup is overflowing!"

The words had barely left my mouth when Dad's fist hit me so hard I crumpled into the trench. He kicked me, dragged me out of the trench, and pulled me to my feet. He continued kicking me while slapping my face several times as hard as he could. Terrified, I wet my pants, but he didn't notice since I was already covered with manure and cow urine. Stunned, I had no idea what had set him off.

"No son of mine is going to talk like a city slicker!" He slapped me several more times on the side of the head. "The water cup is not overflowing; it's running over!" He shoved me back from him when the cow he'd been milking was finished.

Released from his clutches, I staggered out of the barn. My vision was blurred; my head pounded with pain; blood gushed from my nose; my lips had begun to swell. And I couldn't stop crying. In the bitterly cold morning air, my wet clothes stuck to my skin as I stumbled toward the house. I'd climbed up the stairs to the back door before he caught up with me.

"Don't you dare tell your mother, or I'll give you a beating you'll never forget! Straighten up and stop crying, you miserable pantywaist!"

With that he grabbed the garden hose and blasted the manure off my clothing. The icy water bit into my wounds. When he was satisfied that the filth had been washed from my clothing, I slunk into the house, hoping my mom wouldn't see me. I sneaked up to the bedroom I shared with my brothers.

I was terrified of my father's threats. I didn't want to go to school, but I didn't want to stay home either. I didn't want to have to lie to my teachers, and I didn't want to lie to my mother. I longed for someone who would just hold me and let me cry until the pain stopped. If I promised my dad I wouldn't tell mom what happened, couldn't I, at least, let her hold me? But I knew that wasn't feasible because my mother would ask why I was crying. I could run away! How many times had I dreamed of doing just that. But what would happen to me if I were caught and sent back? I might as well face it—I was worthless trash, too stupid to ever amount to anything.

When my father would talk about me to other people, I'd cringe in embarrassment. He'd make fun of me and tell them how much he hated me. "Why, I actually had to teach my worthless son how to 'talk like a man'! I'm not about to have a son of mine talkin' like some sissy!"

The beatings lasted until I was sixteen. The last one caused a black eye, bloody nose, fat lip, and a stream of blood oozing from between my teeth. To top it off, I'd wet my pants. His mistake was forcing me to walk through a group of people in an effort to embarrass me further. His plan backfired. Someone who saw my injuries threatened to report him to the authorities. As a result, he never touched me again, but there were times when he acted as if he wanted to very badly.

Though the beatings stopped, the emotional abuse continued. With every hateful word, he ingrained in me the belief that I would never amount to anything. I was so afraid of failure that I subconsciously set myself up to fail. And fail I did—from completely blanking out on the music I was playing during a performance at boarding school to bumbling through every social contact I tried to make with members of the opposite sex. Around my peers I was shy and easily intimidated. Like the weaker chicken trapped in a pen of healthier chickens, I was the prime target for being heckled. In high school, bullies regularly took their shots at harassing me. I lived in a state of constant terror until I escaped to a Christian boarding school.

During Christmas vacation of my senior year, I welcomed the opportunity to stay at the school rather than go home. By staying at school, I could avoid my father's abuse and also work off part of my bill. Owing nothing at graduation was a bonus as far as I was concerned. I thought this was a good idea until I discovered that my biggest tormentor was also staying at the school. I didn't know which was worse, my father or the bully. Just a month previously, he and a gang of his cronies threw me off the porch of the dormitory into the bushes seven feet below. And now I found myself stuck not only on campus with him but working alone with him for two weeks!

"OK, boys!" Our supervisor pointed toward a boxcar full of redwood two-by-fours. "That's your job. Unload the wood and stack it over by the wall." He pointed toward the yawning cavern of the wood shop. With that he strode off toward his pickup truck. "Call me if you have any problems."

I took a deep breath and glanced out of the corner of my eye at my nemesis. He grinned back at me. From the glint in his eyes, I knew that this would be a long two weeks. The first day was bad. He heckled me incessantly. The second day was like the first.

Halfway through the third day, I'd had it with his jabs. I dropped my armload of lumber and dived for his waist. I had three brothers; I knew how to fight. We regularly wrestled with one another. If we were caught, we would be punished. Because our punishments were always more painful than the actual fight, I avoided fighting as much as possible. But I'd had it with this guy. I couldn't take any more. The perpetual bullying and belittling had to stop!

As we wrestled on the warehouse floor, I was surprised how easily I overpowered him. Within a few short minutes, I'd pinned him to the ground. Lying flat on his back on the concrete floor, he looked up at me and suddenly asked, "Are you a Christian?"

Still holding him down, I froze. "What difference does that make?"

"That's why we've been bugging you. We wanted to see how long you could last and if you are for real."

Oops! Now I felt terrible. I rolled off of him and onto the sawdust-coated floor. "I'm sorry."

"Hey, that's OK." He sat up and brushed the sawdust off his shirt and jeans. "I deserved it. I guess even Christians have a right to defend themselves, right?"

I stared at him for an instant and then broke into laughter. He laughed as well. I stood up and reached out a hand toward him. He took it. I helped him to his feet. This proved to be a turning point for me. I discovered that by laughing with people who laughed at me, I could change their laughter from derisive humor to a joke shared. From then on I quit being afraid of saying or doing the wrong thing socially and, instead, chose to laugh at my own mistakes.

While I made progress socially, I transferred my fear of my father into a terrifying fear of my God. No matter what people told me about the loving heavenly Father, I knew that, in time, He would hurt me too. How could I trust Him? How could I ever be good enough to please Him?

new beginnings

"You are the dumbest kid in the country!" For years I'd heard my dad shout such accusations. Attending college was my way to prove to him and to myself that I wasn't dumb. I wasn't stupid. I could make something of myself! However, I had to work part of the summer after graduation to pay off my academy bill, leaving little time to make enough money for my college entrance fees. Seeing something in me that my dad never saw, my aunt Helen gave me enough money to register for classes in the fall.

During my freshman year, the financial struggle was much worse than at the academy, though my grades were mediocre at best due to my long hours on the job. To make ends meet I worked forty-eight to fifty-six hours a week as an orderly in a local hospital while attending college full time. Regardless of how many hours I put in, the office of finance called me regularly, asking how and when I would be able to pay my bill. Each time I would assure them that by working throughout the following summer months, I would have my bill paid.

I completed my freshman year and charged into an accelerated work schedule. My goal was to pay off my freshman-year bills and save enough to enter school in the fall. After covering my bills and personal expenses each payday, I would take whatever money was left to the college business office and apply it to my outstanding account.

On my way to the office one Friday, I ran into one of my friends' girlfriend. The usually perky little brunette with sparkling brown eyes greeted me with a sad little Hi and then burst into tears.

"What's wrong?" This was bad! My initial reaction was to wrap my arms around her to console her, but she was my friend's girl. I didn't want my friend mad at me. So instead, I kept my arms at my sides.

"I-I-I . . ." She buried her face in her hands.

Not having a clue as how to handle the situation, I clumsily patted her shoulder. From her sniffles, moist cheeks, and runny nose, I could tell she needed a tissue. I didn't have a tissue or handkerchief to offer. I checked my pockets to be certain.

"Listen, let me walk you back to the dorm while you tell me what's wrong."

She nodded and daintily dotted her runny nose against the back of her hand. "Sammy broke up with me this morning." Her statement triggered another bout of tears.

"Oh, I'm so sorry." I'd seen it coming, but I didn't tell her that. "Did he give you a reason?"

She nodded and gestured wildly through her sobs. I listened as best I could, but I didn't understand most of what she said. Once inside the women's residence parlor, she sat on a small two-person love seat. Still wanting to be careful not to cross the perilous line between a caring friend and an emotionally involved confidant, I lowered myself into the matching armchair adjacent to the sofa.

She'd barely resumed her story when a young woman bounded down the stairs and into the residence hall director's office. The excited voice coming from the office diverted my attention from my friend's ex-girlfriend's tale. I struggled to focus on the weeping girl, but couldn't.

"Do you know how to tie a necktie?" Apparently there was a negative response because the anxious young woman burst from the office and accosted a co-ed entering the front door. Again she asked, "Do you know how to tie a necktie?"

The co-ed shook her head and disappeared up the stairs. Curiosity got the best of me. I shot her a surreptitious glance just as she noticed me sitting there. Embarrassed that she'd caught me looking at her, I quickly turned away. Within seconds I sensed her standing by my left shoulder.

"Please . . . can you tie a man's tie?"

Thinking she was asking a trick question, I shrugged. "Sure I can."

"Well then, please, would you tie these ties that way?" She held out two long, lace-edge flaps attached to the collar of her blouse.

I stared at the front of the girl's blouse and groaned inside. What sounded like a simple task was hardly that! I kept my neckties perpetually knotted. Once I'd initially tied a new tie, I would slip it over my head to remove it or to put it on, thus never having to go through the procedure again. In addition, I'd never tied a tie backward! If she could take off the tie and let me tie it around my neck first, I could do it. That wasn't an option since her tie was fastened to her blouse. Suddenly I felt like a bumbling kid again, standing in front of a disapproving school teacher I desperately wanted to please. I answered the girl the only way I could.

"Yes, ma'am." I eyed the offending collar again before taking the two ends of the tie from her hands. The brown-haired, hazel-eyed girl smiled confidently up at me. My hands trembled as I held the two pieces of fabric. This was the closest I'd ever been to a young woman's neck. Sweat beaded on my forehead as I managed to manipulate the silky fabric into a proper gentleman's knot. Certain the color in my face had heightened during the exchange, I straightened the knot about her collar and heaved a sigh of relief.

"There."

Grinning with delight, she whirled about, checked out my knot in a nearby wall mirror and then whirled back to face me. "Perfect! Thank you. Oh yeah, hi! My name's Bonnie Fike." The grateful young woman shot me a coy little smile and held out her hand for me to shake.

"Uh, er, hi. I'm Tom—Tom Sanford."

She lifted one shoulder slightly and batted her beautiful hazel eyes at me. "I have a child psychology class coming up in a few minutes. I'd like it if you'd walk me to class."

Instantly I decided I would walk this girl wherever she wanted to go. Then I remembered my friend's ex-girlfriend. My heart sank. I couldn't just abandon her. Slowly I turned toward the sofa. She was gone. I shrugged my shoulders in relief. Oh well, help one damsel in distress and lose the other damsel.

"Sure."

As we strolled across the parklike campus, we talked, but I have no idea about the topic. I just knew that this lovely creature by my side cared about what I had to say. That fact alone would have stolen my heart. Unfortunately, fifteen minutes after we parted company, I'd forgotten her name. Now I was in a real pickle. We'd been attracted to one another. Even I knew that. And I definitely wanted to see her again, but not knowing her name, how would I ever find her?

Over the next two weeks I couldn't get the bright-eyed brunette off my mind. I had to see her again, but how? The only thing I could think to do was to wander around campus and hope I'd run into her. Having a rare afternoon when I didn't have to be at work, I first went to the women's residence. Being too shy to ask any questions, I hung around for a few minutes, and then headed for the student lounge. At least there I wouldn't look like some stalker lurking in the shadows. The girl of my dreams wasn't there either. Thinking she might be sitting on one of the benches around campus, I prowled from one tree-covered walkway to the next until I'd covered every inch of the campus.

This is hopeless! I sat down on the nearest stone bench and buried my head in my hands. I've lost her forever! How could I be so stupid as to forget her name? If I were taking summer classes, where might I be? I was about to abandon my search when I thought of checking the library. New vigor surged through me. I sprinted to the campus library. Once there, I searched every nook and study carrel on the first floor—

nothing. I did the same on the second floor—nothing. I suppose she could be on the third floor. As I headed for the stairs, I spied one lone female student sitting at a desk near the door. She wore glasses and was hunched over, writing something in a notebook. I knew my mystery girl didn't wear glasses, but I'd check this student out anyway. The girl looked up, removed her glasses, and smiled. I blinked in amazement. There she was—right in front of me.

"Uh, hi." Trying to act cool, I gave her a friendly wave. If only I could recall her name!

"Hi, yourself." She gestured me toward the chair on the opposite side of the table. "I was just thinking about you." Her eyes twinkled with delight. She shoved her notebook across the desk at me. There on the page she'd written "Tom Sanford" several times.

Whoa! She'd been thinking about me? How can I convince her that I'd been thinking about her too if I can't even remember her name? I shrugged off my moment of confusion and grinned at her. "What are you studying?"

She slid a paperback textbook in my direction. Whoopee! I heaved a sigh of relief. While the textbook itself looked respectably boring, I'd lucked out. In the upper right-hand corner of the cover she'd written her name—Bonnie Fike. Yes! That's it. Bonnie Fike! I vowed to myself that I'd not forget her name a second time.

Flush with victory, I knew I couldn't let this moment pass. "So are you doing anything tomorrow night?" I groaned to myself at my lack of style and creativity. "If not, would you like to do something to-gether?"

Her face lit up with the most beautiful smile I could have imagined. "Yes, I'd love to."

Now I was in trouble. What did people do on dates? I was a country boy. I had no idea. I'd never been on a real date. Stumbling around my repertoire of things to do and places to go, I remembered that it was Tuesday, which would make tomorrow Wednesday. "How about prayer meeting?"

She smiled again. "I'd like that."

"Great. I'll come by the dorm around seven-fifteen to pick you up."

"I'll be ready."

Now I had another problem. School rules demanded that I bring along a chaperone in order for a young lady to ride with me in my car. Remembering the stern threats of the dean of women, I decided I'd try to convince my little sister to come with me. After we picked up my date, I'd drop little sis off at home before going to the church. Everything went smoothly that evening. I felt like a pro by the time I took Bonnie back to the dorm. Before saying good night, I suggested we date again on the weekend.

On Sabbath, date number two included the church service, sunshine band, detention home, jail band, and finally the county home band concert, giving me just enough time to get her back to the dormitory before curfew. What a woman! I couldn't believe my good fortune. Finding Bonnie, I knew I'd been truly blessed. On Wednesday I eagerly dressed for our third date—another prayer-meeting date.

Following prayer meeting, Bonnie was extra quiet on the way back to campus. "Can we stop and talk?" Her eyes lacked their normal sparkle.

"Sure." I pulled the car onto the shoulder of the road and parked. My heart sank. This can't be good. "What is it?" I steeled myself for the fateful "I don't want to get serious right now, can we be friends?" speech that my buddies had so often talked about.

"Well, as you know, the summer school session is almost over. But what you might not know is, in a few days I'll be heading to Green Bay, Wisconsin, to teach . . ." She glanced down at her folded hands and then back at me. "Will I ever see you again?"

I felt like I'd been kicked in the stomach. She'd barely entered my life, and now she'd be heading out! Since there had always been several people around whenever we went on a date, we hadn't had much time to talk privately. Like it or not, she was leaving and I was staying. I couldn't let her just go! I really cared for this woman, a whole lot! Had I made a mistake of not spending more time alone with her? Was she going to tell me something I didn't want to hear? Would this be our last goodbye? I just couldn't let that happen!

Then a revolutionary new thought entered my mind. *What if I ask her to marry me? There's a fifty-fifty chance. Either she'll say yes or she'll say no. If she says no, well, Green Bay is a long distance away. At least I won't be embarrassed if she tells all of her friends about what I did. If she says yes, then we'll have time during our engagement to get to know one another better. So, what do I have to lose? It's worth a try.*

But then reason set in. *Wait a minute. What am I thinking? We've only had three dates. But I think I love her*—as much as I knew about love. Taking a deep breath, I decided to go for it. To avoid eye contact, just in case she rejected me, I stared straight ahead, at the empty, open road in front of the car. "Bonnie, will you marry me?"

A mere second of silence passed. Suddenly Bonnie grabbed me by the jacket collar, turned my face toward hers, and planted a big kiss on my lips. "Oh, Tom, I will make you the happiest man in the world!"

Two years later we were married, though I hadn't finished college at the time. Up to that point I'd been in college for three years, and at the rate I was going, it would take another five to graduate. But Bonnie was determined to earn her PHT—Putting Hubby Through. In the end, it took me only another three years to graduate.

From the very beginning of our marriage, people began sending kids to us to care for, sometimes for a day, other times for a week. Grandparents needing a respite from the demands of raising a second set of youngsters would ask us to take their loved ones for a short time.

I wondered why we were chosen to take these children. I didn't see any of my neighbors caring for other people's children. It was almost as if God had a plan for us, but I wasn't sure what it might be. I figured that once I'd finished college, we'd move on and this "intrusion" into our marriage would end.

Looking back, I can see that the special times we spent with troubled children were the more treasured moments in our fledgling marriage. Bonnie and I made it a point to do things with our young guests that we were never allowed to do or were scolded for doing when we were younger.

Actually, our first guest wasn't human at all. It was a Saint Bernard puppy named Dobbie. Perhaps Dobbie was the Lord's way of preparing us for things to come. The critter chewed everything in sight—our shoes, our boots, even our neighbor's shoes. I was convinced that if the tires on the car weren't so big, he would have chewed through them as well. But we loved Dobbie just the same. Like most big dogs, he enjoyed riding in the car with his head outside of the open window. Fortunately for us, his slobber blew backward. (I always did wonder why passing drivers would shake their fists at us.)

After Dobbie came the children—first one, then another, and then a continual stream. We would take them to the dunes on Lake Michigan, where we would play in the sand. We could build the most amazing sand castles and forts. More often than not, our car would get stuck, and we'd have to push it out of the loose sand. But it didn't matter. We'd had too much fun to allow such a little inconvenience to ruin our day.

Other times we'd go boating or water skiing. Some Sabbath afternoons, we'd take them to the park. Bonnie and I would join them, swinging on the swings and sliding down the slides. In the winter, since we were too poor to own a sled, we'd slide down hills on flattened cardboard boxes.

The children loved it! I loved it! It was the first time in my life when I didn't have to worry every minute about being punished for what I was doing wrong—or for just being, for that matter. Finally I had room to breathe and to grow. And even though the feeling of freedom didn't last beyond the event, it certainly felt good while it lasted.

The first child we took into our home was deaf. Communicating with him proved difficult because neither Bonnie nor I knew sign language. He'd been abused because he was different and couldn't hear. His abuse had been so bad that he would scream with fright over any movement after dark, from the curtains blowing in the breeze to the shadows cast by the moon on its journey across the night sky.

Both of us understood his situation and were extra cautious when dealing with him. For me, his fears were almost a déjà vu. We knew his life had been rough to this point and would be rough from here on out. So while he was in our home, we loved giving him as many opportunities as possible to enjoy his fleeting moments of childhood.

In the fall of 1966 while I was still in school, Bonnie was hired to teach third grade in a public school outside Benton Harbor, Michigan. Located in a low-income neighborhood known for racial violence, the school struggled to survive. It was common knowledge that many parents attended the PTA meetings with the express purpose of picking fights with another child's parents. It wasn't uncommon to see father A fighting with father B and mother B brawling out back of the school with mother A. Unfortunately, teachers weren't exempt from receiving a parent's verbal abuse.

At the end of Bonnie's first semester there, the principal asked me if I would teach fourth grade. The students in the fourth-grade room had already run off two teachers within three months, and the principal needed someone to finish out the term. Because I was still in college, I felt honored to be asked. Little did I know . . .

The first day I walked into the large room where I would teach and glanced about the space the other teachers had abandoned. I could see why. The scene was chaotic. The room had been divided in half with a folding curtain. Located on the other side of the curtain, Bonnie's third-grade classroom was the epitome of order and calm. From the first day of second-semester's classes, I could hear almost all that went on in her space from my side of the folding curtain. Occasionally, when my world seemed to be blowing part, I would peek between the curtains to enjoy the respite that comes from watching children learn.

My classroom, on the other hand, was absolute bedlam. I wondered, do children change so dramatically between third and fourth grade? The principal assured me that this particular class had been a bad mix since first grade. Being a country boy, I had no idea that children as young as fourth grade could be so tough and that they'd already established themselves in street gangs. The children came from desperately poor homes. Many of them brought two slices of bread filled with canned dog food for lunch. My heart ached for them, but my nerves were frazzled! It was almost as if I were being abused again, but by the other end of the age spectrum.

One day four of my boys failed to return from recess. Ordering the rest of the class to remain in their seats at threat of extra homework, I searched for my errant boys. I found them in the bathroom, waiting to attack me with knives. As I walked through the door, I found myself surrounded by four shiny switchblades aimed at my chest. Instinctively, I employed my best "Terminator—all right, who's first?" stance and literally threw them out of the bathroom one at a time.

"Now get back to the classroom!" I called after the last terrified boy leaped through the door and bounded down the hallway toward the classroom.

A few days later the president of the PTA called me on the phone. "Tom, I don't know how to tell you this, but I just got off the phone from speaking with the mother of one of your boys." He named the boy. "She swears that she is going to sue you. She said that her son came home from school, black and blue from head to toe."

"What?" I couldn't believe it. *Good luck on the lawsuit. Bonnie and I don't have two dimes to rub together.* I chuckled to myself even as I thought back to the incident in question. There was no way the little monster had suffered that many bruises at my hand!

Before I could come up with an appropriate response, he continued. "I know it's not your fault, Tom. These people are just looking to make money off of somebody. Besides I saw the guy playing football afterward. His bruises came from playing football, not from being tossed out of the boys' room on his ear."

Relieved, I hung up the telephone. *Maybe, just maybe I will survive the semester in one piece. Abused kids in our home and, now, a fourth-grade class of troublemakers! What is this all about anyway? Is God setting me up for something? If He is, I wish He'd get to the point! Then again, maybe this will all pass.* I'd go back and finish college, and then find a quiet little country parish where I could preach the Word of God to a congregation of aging, blue-haired ladies whose greatest temptation was to gossip over the back fence or watch their favorite soap operas.

I convinced myself that the issues these kids faced resulted from a local situation, and that their problems were unique to the area. Yet if I'd been honest with myself, I would have had to admit that I, too, had been one of those troubled, hurting, and abused kids. Ignoring the facts didn't make it go away. How many times over the years had my dad told me how much he hated me? Even when I was fifty-five years old, he wrote a letter to me saying I was "no son of his."

I wasn't yet ready to accept the fact that God could use my dysfunctional childhood to help others. I wasn't yet ready to face myself in the mirror of a teenager's turbulent life.

ghosts of the past

Grateful to have escaped the classroom and the emotional issues that stemmed from dealing with difficult children, I found work framing houses and returned to college part time in the fall. But while changing my employment might have helped me avoid many of the issues from my childhood, other problems from my past still loomed bigger than life in my present—for instance, doing laundry at the laundromat. Before I married Bonnie, I did my laundry at the local laundromat between two and three in the morning, when no one was around. I was embarrassed to fold my underwear in front of other people. Believing doing the laundry was women's work, I didn't expect to have to do the family laundry ever again once I got married—especially having to do the laundry at a public laundromat. However, the day came when Bonnie became sick, and she asked me to do the laundry. Immediately I eyed the clock. It was midafternoon on Sunday. The local laundromat would be teeming with housewives doing the family wash. I looked back at Bonnie and shook my head in a half-hearted, "Please don't ask me to do this" gesture. She was serious.

My father had ingrained in me a clear demarcation between men's roles and women's roles. Part of his psychological abuse was to make me do *wounded healer*

"women's work"—wash dishes, baby-sit my little sister, and other household duties, all the while calling me a sissy for doing it. I had three brothers, but I was the one "stuck" doing the women's work in our home. When I finally was allowed to work outside on the farm, he relegated me to driving the team of horses rather than operating a tractor because "tractors are for men!" Thus when I became an adult—a "real man"—I believed I would never again have to do the dishes, the laundry, or any of the various other household tasks that my father had deemed "women's work." I'd have a wife to do those things. But now my wife was sick. She needed my help. While I loved her dearly, I hated the dreaded task of doing the laundry!

"Please, Tom, I really am too sick to go anywhere, and you've run out of clean socks and underwear." Bonnie did look pale and peaked.

"Bonnie, I've never in my life gone to the laundromat in the middle of the day!" I was thinking, *Worse yet, I've never washed and folded ladies' unmentionables in public either!*

She sighed. I could see she felt miserable. "Sorry, but if you want clean clothes tomorrow, you're going to have to do the laundry today."

I wanted to please Bonnie, and I felt guilty for being so bullheaded, so I capitulated. "Oh, all right!"

Patiently she gave me clear instructions to measure out a quarter of a cup of soap for each load. I assured her that I understood. "Just rest and get better. I can handle it."

As she stumbled back to bed she mumbled something about the water being soft. Since I'd done laundry before, I smugly half-ignored her instructions. When I got to the laundromat, I found that my nightmare had come true. I found lots of people doing their laundry in the middle of the day. Flustered, I sneaked into the building as inconspicuously as I could and found an empty washing machine. Checking to make certain no one was watching me, I stuffed Bonnie's unmentionables into the front-loading washer along with mine.

Pleased that I'd gotten them all in the same machine, I closed the door, dropped the quarters into the slot and measured out a quarter cup of soap. I eyed the measuring cup. *Hmm, sure isn't much soap in a quarter cup.* I checked the measurements again. *Yep, it's exactly one-*

quarter cup. I peered through the glass in the door of the machine. *That can't possibly be enough soap for all those clothes!*

Before we had married, I'd always used the pre-measured packs of detergent—no measuring. Having a gallon bucket of soap was a new experience for me.

Deciding that a quarter cup would never adequately clean the entire load, I added an extra half a cup. Then I had another thought. *If soap is supposed to get things clean, then more soap should get them really clean, right?* I tossed in another half a cup of detergent. Satisfied with my logic, I closed the door and turned the knob to start the machine. The growling beast churned to life on command.

I gazed about the crowded facility. The faces of my fellow launderers were glued to a variety of magazines—*Woman's Day, Newsweek, Ladies' Home Journal.* To better blend in, I chose a "manly" sports magazine from the stack on a small metal folding table. I'd barely browsed past the table of contents when a gigantic explosion filled the crowded room. I looked up and followed everyone's gaze to my machine.

A deluge of bubbles spewed out of the open door of the machine with what seemed the force of Niagara Falls. The tile on the floor surrounding the machine was mattress deep in white suds. Humiliated, I tried to decide what to do. I couldn't claim the clothes as mine, not with everyone watching! But I needed the clothes! Well, I'd just have to buy new clothing. Feeling the noose of disgrace tightening around my neck, I tossed the magazine on the empty chair beside me and rushed toward the exit.

In my haste to escape, I slipped on the soapy water, landed on my backside, and skidded to a stop beneath the folding table. The room erupted in raucous laughter. The manager gingerly made his way to me and asked if I was injured. I assured him that only my dignity had been damaged. As he helped me to my feet, he asked if the clothes inside the belching machine were mine.

"Yes, sir," I mumbled, hoping no one else could hear my reply.

But he took care of that. In a loud, booming voice he said, "Fine. Let me get you a mop, a bucket"—and after glancing once more at the mess mushrooming at our feet—"and a shovel," he teased. "Here! Get busy."

I stared in horror. I couldn't have made more of a spectacle of myself if I had tried. I was mortified beyond reason. The other customers put down their magazines to watch me mop up the soapy water. No one offered to help me; they merely watched, whispered, and snickered. When I'd finally corralled the last soap bubble and soaked up the final puddle of water, the manager gave me enough quarters to rinse the load of wash still waiting in the machine.

Later I staggered into the house like I'd just endured my first day at boot camp and promptly announced to my sick wife that I was never, ever, ever, going to do the laundry again in my entire life! "From now on, the laundry is your responsibility. I don't want to know anything about it!"

I proceeded to tell her my sordid tale of woe, expecting at least one word of tender sympathy from her. When she finally stopped laughing, her words of wisdom grated against my wounded pride. "Looks like that was a good lesson about following instructions, don't you think?"

Months later I had all but forgotten my mortification at the laundromat when Bonnie again asked me to do the weekly laundry. This time she was recovering from the flu.

Visions of a volcano of soap bubbles popped into my head. "No way! You know how I feel about doing laundry. No! No! I would rather wait until tomorrow or go buy all new clothes!"

"Honey, we can't afford to buy all new clothes." Her indulgent smile irked me.

"I'd rather steal them!" I was not going to the laundromat during the daytime ever again!

She chuckled in spite of her condition. "Look, we really need the clothes washed. Would you do it if you could wash them after dark?"

I thought for a moment. One look at my wife's distressed face and I caved in. I waited until ten that night before I bundled the canvas bags of soiled clothing into the car and drove downtown. Once there, I cruised by the laundromat to be certain the place was vacant. When I'd assured myself no one was around, I dragged the bags inside the establishment and stuffed the clothing into the nearest machine. This time I measured the soap accurately and started the machine without a hitch. I immediately left the premises in case someone came in and identified me as the jerk who had made the previous mess. With nothing to do for the next forty-five minutes, I drove to the college to see a buddy of mine. He was coming out of the dorm when I arrived. I waved him down, and he came over to my car. While we were talking, a carload of ruffians drove up behind my car.

The driver parked, got out of his vehicle, and strolled up to where my friend and I stood. His three buddies did the same.

"Got a cigarette?"

"Sorry, I don't smoke." I eyed his stained blue jeans and scruffy T-shirt.

"Got a match?"

"Sorry!"

"Hey, you think you're a wise guy? We should beat you up just for the principle of the thing." His buddies seconded his proclamation. Now I knew I looked much younger than my age, but I was a married man of twenty-four, and they were just teenagers. But standing next to me, these big guys made me feel like David in a grove of giants. These guys were picking a fight, but I wasn't so inclined. I tried to reason with him.

"How would beating us up benefit you? All it would do is hurt us and send you to jail." My logic stopped the ringleader in his tracks.

"Well, you'd better get out of here before I change my mind," the driver snarled. "And don't call the police, or we'll hunt you down and kill you!"

My friend and I hopped into my car. I revved the engine and peeled out as fast as my car could go. Unfortunately, during our speedy getaway, I spun gravel. I didn't realize it at the time, but a rock flew up and cracked the other car's windshield. Suddenly the chase was on. We raced through the countryside and back again. Just when I thought I'd lost them, I remembered my wet laundry waiting for me at the laundromat.

"I have to stop at the laundromat to transfer my wash to a dryer."

"Great!"

"Sorry!" I turned down the side street leading to the laundromat. Once there, I transferred the clothes into a dryer while my friend found a magazine to occupy his time. The more I thought about our encounter with the teenage thugs, the wiser it seemed to call the police in case they came back to hassle us again. Looking around for a pay phone, I spotted a booth across the street.

"You know, I think I'd better report those guys to the police—just to be safe." I jangled the pocketful of change I still had in my pocket. "I'll be right back."

My friend nodded and settled himself in one of the hard plastic chairs. I stepped out on the empty street and glanced about. Assuring myself that no one was around, I walked across the street and placed my call. While I reported the gist of my confrontation with the thugs to the police dispatcher, a familiar vehicle turned the corner and drove slowly toward me. My heart stopped when they spotted my car parked in front of the laundromat. They whipped into a parking space and bounded inside the laundromat. Seconds later they came out of the building, looked around, and started to get into their car, but then they spotted me in the phone booth. My friend followed at a distance. My heart leaped into my throat—the two of us couldn't ward off the four of them.

"Please hurry! The kids just came out of the laundromat and they are heading my way!"

"Sir, what did you do to provoke them?" I didn't like the dispatcher's attitude.

"Nothing, they're just looking for a fight." I wasn't sure I'd convinced her of my innocence. "Please hurry!" As I hung up the receiver the leader muscled open the door of the phone booth.

"Who did you call?"

Fearing their earlier threat might come true, I said, "My mother." Ah, the hazards of lying! He didn't appreciate my attempt at humor. With one walloping punch, he flattened me against the backside of the telephone booth. I saw stars. He hit my face so hard he almost knocked me out. Somehow I found the presence of mind to slam the door closed with my foot. The four guys pounded on the glass until I was certain it would shatter. When it didn't give, they turned on my friend.

Before I could rush to his aid, the arrival of a patrol car saved us from serious and certain injury. The officers took one look at my face and ticketed the four young men for assault and battery. In a move to escape punishment, they begged me to forgive them.

"We'll never do this again," the leader vowed. "Please don't press charges."

I was in a quandary. The kid looked so remorseful. My heart wanted to release them. After all, I hadn't been hurt too badly, and I'd had worse beatings from my own father.

One of the officers recognized my weakening resolve. "Don't let them off. If you do, they'll just hurt someone else."

"Yeah," the other officer volunteered. "They've been harassing folks all over the county. Ya' gotta' press charges. Someone has to stop them before they do serious damage to someone."

I studied the faces of the four young men, and again, I saw my dad mirrored in their angry eyes. I shrugged. I couldn't change the lives of these guys.

Why me? I asked myself. Within the first year of marriage I'd accepted abused kids into our home, faced a classroom of unruly nine-year-olds, and now, these guys. And oh yes, my fat lip is going to look great in front of thirty-two recalcitrant fourth-graders tomorrow! The last thought solidified my decision. I turned toward the policeman.

"Go ahead; book 'em. I'll press charges."

* * *

At the end of the school term, I'd resisted the flattering offer of the principal to teach fifth grade the next term. Would I like to follow the little darlings, grade by grade to graduation? Pastoring a "little brown church in the wildwood" was sounding better and better.

I chose not to return to the classroom the next year. But leaving teaching meant no extra paycheck coming in each month—that hurt. We'd been asking God for the direction He would have us go. I believed the promise in Proverbs 3: "In all thy ways acknowledge him, and he shall direct thy paths," but I hadn't seen the evidence of it until I was driving through Berrien Springs, Michigan, one day and spotted a "For Lease" sign on a filling station. I called the gas company and told them I'd like to lease the station. Before I had time to think twice, I met with their representative to write up the lease.

"You will be required to put down one hundred dollars. We will fill your tanks. At the end of the first month, you will pay us what fuel you used. By the way, what are your hours going to be?"

"Twenty-four hours a day, six days a week."

He arched an eyebrow at me and ripped up the partially written contract. "Forget it. If you don't open on Saturdays, you'll go broke. The previous people who leased the place grossed less than two thousand dollars a month. And they were open seven days a week. They couldn't support their family on what was left."

"I can't run a gas station on God's holy Sabbath. I believe it's important to stay closed on Saturdays." I leaned back and ran one hand over my stubble of a beard. "The way I look at it, if I obey the Lord, He will take care of me."

"Don't you understand the weekends are the busiest days of the week? And you have competition with two other stations on the same intersection. You won't make it!"

I shrugged my shoulders and smiled. "We'll see."

"OK, it's your funeral. I'll take your hundred dollars and write you up a contract. But I want you to know that I'll be back at the end of the month to close you down because you aren't going to make it!"

The salesman's prediction of failure didn't sit well with me. I was determined to prove him wrong. So I bought a semi load of watermelons and had them delivered to the station. For every purchase of ten gallons or more, I gave away a free watermelon. At the end of the first month, I'd grossed twenty thousand dollars in sales. I couldn't have been more pleased.

By now Bonnie was back teaching school full time. I was attending classes part time and operating the station in the black. I had ten employees working for me. For the first time in my life, things seemed to be going well. One quiet afternoon when no one else was around, I was lounging on a folding chair in front of the station, studying for a pop quiz, when a young man suddenly appeared in front of me and asked me for a cigarette.

Barely looking up from the textbook I was studying, I said, "I'm sorry, but the gas station doesn't sell cigarettes." When I looked up, my smile dissolved into a curious look of recognition. It was one of the teens who'd assaulted me months earlier.

He glared down at me. "Look buddy! You should know that I am out to get you!" With that he stormed off, unaware that I'd leased the station and also that I was alone at the time.

What was he doing out on the street so soon? I called the local district attorney and was told that the boys' numbers were at the top of the draft list.

"They're heading off to the military in a short time. They won't be bothering you anymore." I was relieved. I'd once again been spared coming into contact with a bunch of troubled teens.

Seven months later, I received a letter from Uncle Sam telling me that the draft board couldn't figure out if my purpose was to get a college degree or run a business. They didn't ask me. Instead, they decided that because I was attending classes only part time, my business was my greater priority. I was drafted and ordered to appear in Chicago for my physical.

Because I was planning on entering the ministry and scheduled to graduate in three months, I went to see the intimidating "matriarch" of the theological seminary. I asked her to put me on the list of ministerial students to be interviewed by conference presidents looking for interns.

She shook her head so forcefully I thought I'd asked the wrong question. "Sorry, but we have so many ministerial interns already on the list. And we have more applications than jobs."

"Would you at least put my name on the list, please?" To get rid of me, she complied.

Shortly thereafter, early one Sunday morning, the phone rang. It was the seminary "matriarch." Her message was brief and exciting. "The president of the Montana Conference of Seventh-day Adventists is here on campus and wants to speak with you."

wagons west

Chapter 4

Bonnie and I were still in bed the Sunday morning the phone call came. We'd been out with friends the evening before. Electrified into action, I hopped out of bed and ran into the bathroom. In my haste to shave, I nicked myself several times. The beads of blood looked a lot like pimples. *Great! Just what I need—to look younger than ever!* My youthful appearance frequently complicated my life.

So like all red-blooded males would do in similar circumstances, I staunched the bleeding with tiny pieces of toilet paper. After running a comb through my hair, I dressed in a clean pullover shirt and a pair of blue jeans and then drove to the seminary. As I pulled into the seminary parking area, I caught a glimpse of myself in the rearview mirror; my face was still dotted with toilet paper. Relieved I'd spotted the paper before I shook hands with the visiting conference president, I gingerly removed each, took a deep breath, and hurried inside the building.

The seminary "matriarch" looked me up and down, her disapproval obvious, before motioning me down the hall to the room where the Montana Conference president was waiting. When I reached the door, I knocked and entered at his bidding. He motioned me to a chair. We visited for a few minutes, and he asked me about my conversion experience, my spiritual commitment, and my stance on several theological questions. Looking satisfied with my responses, he leaned back in his chair.

"Do you play a musical instrument?" he asked.

"No."

"Do you sing?"

"No."

"What do you do?"

I grinned. "I have a big mouth, if that's any consolation."

He didn't seem impressed with my attempt at humor. My shoulders sank an inch or two. *Oh no, I blew it again.*

"I'd like to speak with your wife, if I may."

I brightened. If anyone could rescue the wobbly interview, Bonnie could.

"Perhaps we could go over to your place, after you give her fair warning, of course."

He glanced toward the phone and then back at me. I nodded. "Oh, yes, I'll give her a call and let her know we're coming."

Fretting over my every word and gesture, I offered to drive my car. He suggested that he follow me in his own vehicle. By the time I opened the front door and ushered the man into our two-bedroom duplex, Bonnie was dressed in her prettiest Sunday morning casuals. Neither of us were dressed to match our visitor's neatly pressed suit and tie. Bonnie, always ready to welcome company, had the apartment shipshape. She invited the conference president to make himself comfortable on the sofa while she served him a glass of ice-cold lemonade. Once she completed her hospitality duties, she sat down in the armchair across from where he sat. Silently watching and listening as they chatted for several minutes, I was amazed at how well the interview was going. And then he asked Bonnie the same questions he'd asked me. "Do you play any musical instruments?"

"No, sir." She didn't blink an eyelash.

"Do you sing?"

"No." Her reply was short and direct.

"Uh, what do you do?"

"I'm a grade-school teacher." She smiled and relaxed the tension in her hands folded on her lap.

"You're a teacher?" Instantly he brightened. "Teaching and preaching are a good combination for a ministerial couple." Abruptly he rose to his feet and handed her his empty tumbler. "Thank you so much for meeting with me on such a short notice, Mrs. Sanford. I wish you both well in finding the position God has in mind for you." After he bade us goodbye and left, we simply looked at each other and shrugged.

Throughout the rest of the morning, I relived the interview—word by word—repeatedly kicking myself for all the real and imagined mistakes I'd made. I'd blown the interview. I was certain of it.

"Honey." Bonnie took my clenched hands in hers. "It's in God's hands now. If He wants you to go to Montana, you'll go. You can't change anything."

I knew she was right, but that didn't ease my stress. My father's negative barbs tumbled through my mind—*loser, wimp, worthless.* By noon I was an emotional mess. Bonnie and I had just sat down to a light lunch when the "matriarch" phoned again.

"Mr. Sanford, I want to see you right away!"

I brightened. I assured her that I would be right over to the seminary. I hung up the phone and beamed at Bonnie. "The 'matriarch' wants to see me. It must be good news!"

I bounded up the steps of the building as blissfully unaware as a lamb to the slaughter. At her desk I reached out my hand to greet her only to receive a thin-lipped glare.

"Mr. Sanford! I am disappointed in you, showing up for an interview in your work clothes, looking as if you'd just climbed out of bed!" (I had—but I didn't tell her so.) "I have never been so embarrassed by one of our seminary students in all my years in this office!"

Shifting from foot to foot, I emotionally shrank two inches right before her eyes.

"You will never get a call to the Montana Conference after coming to your interview dressed as you were. You showed a total disregard for the position of the conference president and for the reputation of the ministry! If you ever—and I do mean *if*—want to get a pastoral call, you will arrive for your interview wearing a dark suit, white shirt, and a plain tie. Is that understood?"

I nodded numbly.

"And, furthermore, your shoes must be polished!" She glared as if daring me to protest or make an excuse for my behavior. As I stood there feeling like a bumbling clown, I wondered if getting a pastoral call was the equivalent of signing up for military service.

I returned home feeling dejected and defeated. And I wondered if anyone would ever hire me as a pastor. *My father was right. I am a bumbling loser!* Bonnie comforted me, assuring me that while the first interview might not have gone as I wished, there would be others, and I would do better next time.

During the next couple of weeks I received three calls: one from Newfoundland, one from North Dakota, and, surprise of surprise, a call from Montana. The first thing I did was rush to the encyclopedia to check out the weather conditions in each place. They were all places with long, cold winters.

Having been told I would never get a call because of my casual attire at the interview, I asked the Montana Conference president why he chose me. His answer astonished me: "Because you were the only one who didn't dress up to show off. I think you'll fit in well with the people of Montana."

So we were off to the wild, wild state of Montana. As a thirteen-year-old, my parents had moved us from Pennsylvania to Wisconsin. At the time, my friends and I thought I was moving to the wild West. I expected that we would live primitively and have frequent contact with Native Americans. Of course, that didn't happen.

Now, with our decision made to take the call to Montana, I had misgivings about moving even farther west. Bonnie did too. This time we would cross the Mississippi River! I'd never before been beyond the Mississippi. We drove across the span of muddy water and the mosquito-infested wetlands and entered Minnesota. Then we began an endless climb up the long sweep of road up from the river. Halfway to the top we came upon a semi-truck and trailer slowly inching its way down toward us. As we neared the vehicle, something or Someone jerked the steering wheel out of my hands. The car swerved sharply to the right and off the road onto a flat area along the shoulder. It was as if I had hit a rock with my front tire.

No sooner had our car reached the shoulder than one of the truck's wheels came off and rolled—bouncing like a basketball—down our side of the road. Stunned, we watched as it bounded through the traffic lane where our car would have been if our car hadn't swerved off the road. The truck wheel careened farther down the road, jumped a guard-rail, and quickly disappeared over a hill.

I looked at Bonnie; she looked at me. We both recognized how blessed we were. I climbed out of the car, intent on finding what had pulled us off the road. I found a man standing beside our car. I hadn't seen him there before.

"Thank you so much," he said, "for pulling off the road like that. For some reason I was impressed to follow you. I too would have been in the path of that deadly wheel!"

I assured him that it wasn't my choice. "I must have hit a rock or something." We looked around and could find no rock. I then checked my car and found no sign of an impact or steering damage. The stranger and I stood beside a road neither of us had ever driven before, and together we thanked the Lord for His protection. Then I climbed back into our car, eased back onto the highway, and continued west.

In spite of this dramatic miracle, our dismay increased the farther west we traveled. The lack of trees on the North Dakota prairie made it seem as if we were on a distant planet. By the time we crossed the state line into Montana, we both were questioning whether the Lord could possibly be leading us to such a barren location.

"Maybe taking the call to Montana was a mistake! North Dakota certainly wasn't a good option, and certainly Nova Scotia, with all its fog, wouldn't have been interesting to say the least! Can't we go back to Wisconsin?" Bonnie cast me a pleading look.

I glanced at her worried face and laughed nervously, hoping to ease her tension as well as my own. This wasn't like her. What if we really didn't like living in Montana? Not knowing what else to do, I kept driving. The last tree we saw was in a national forest, east of Jordan, Montana. And I do mean tree.

The terrain, along with our mood, improved the nearer we got to Lewistown, in central Montana, and the Judith Mountains. The tree-covered mountains and the tree-lined streets in the friendly little town welcomed us to our first pastorate.

Not having been born and raised in the home of a pastor or other church employee, I knew very little about how the church worked. I just knew I wanted to work hard to meet my parishioners' needs. It wasn't long before people began asking us to relieve them of their grandchildren on weekends. *Wait a minute,* I wondered. *Is this in a pastor's job description? I thought I left all this behind in Michigan!*

I guess it all started with a visit to a ghost town named Roy, fifty miles from Lewistown, where an old prospector resided. The man had remained in the town once the gold mines played out. I hadn't been there long before we got on the subject of cars, a mutual interest. He took me on a tour of his abandoned auto shop.

"In the twenties, Roy was a booming gold-and-oil town. I ran the local car dealership," the old man told us. We stepped gingerly inside his garage with the caved-in roof. Scattered around the space were antiques of all sorts—motorcycles, safes, and bicycles. In the center of the floor was a vehicle draped with a plastic tarp.

He hauled back the tarp to reveal a mint condition, vintage car. "Some company bought this 1925 Model T touring pickup from me. They drove it to Lewistown and back, parked it, and walked away. They've never come back for it. It hasn't been moved since!" All four tires were flat and the paint was dulled by a half-century of dust; otherwise it was a beautiful piece of machinery. He listened with pride while I appropriately *oohed* and *aahed* over the vehicle. But there was more to see. He led me outside, behind the garage where a 1927 Whippet caught my eye. His aunt and uncle had purchased the vehicle new off the showroom floor and had driven it until 1949 when, because of their advancing age, they left it where it sat.

"Whew! That's quite the car!" I beamed with admiration. Over the years I'd picked up a few mechanical skills and had restored the '36 Chevy I drove while in college. I could see that the Whippet was one special vehicle. "How much would you take for the car?"

"One hundred dollars. I'm tired of having these old cars take up my pasture space."

I examined the vehicle intently. In its present condition I knew the car wouldn't run. "That sounds like a fair price. If I give you a hundred dollars for it, do you have a farm truck with a lift that I could borrow to help me get it back to town?"

"Sure do." He pointed toward a truck standing beside his home. After I gave him the money, I loaded the car onto the truck as if it were my most valuable possession and drove back to town. On the way I stopped at a gas station to see if the tires would hold air. If they did, it would make it easier to get the car off the truck. I filled each tire with air. To my surprise, every one of them remained firm. Pleased with myself, I climbed back into the truck and pulled into traffic. At the next traffic light, I heard a loud bang.

Startled, I saw people on the sidewalk ducking for cover. *Talk about being in the wild West!* A second explosion shook the closest of the store windows. People were no longer running for cover, but were pointing at me and laughing. A third explosion had everyone doubled over with laughter. After the fourth explosion I checked my rearview mirror. My "new" car was slowly slumping down one corner at a time. The aging rubber of the tires couldn't handle the air pressure.

I'd barely pulled into my driveway when the phone began to ring. I received phone calls from people who'd seen me bring my car into town. After laughing about the exploding tires, one caller said, "You know, I've got this grandson who needs something to do to keep him out of trouble. Could you use some help restoring your new old car?"

Right! Just what I want to do—baby-sit a teenager! Not knowing how to say no graciously, I mumbled, "He can help me work on the car for a while." Over the next few months, Danny helped me dismantle the Whippet down to its frame. During the hours of sharing our mutual admiration for the car, I decided that picking up where I'd left off in Michigan was not as bad an idea as I thought. Other parents and grandparents called, asking if Bonnie and I would help with their children as well.

Being a young pastor had a unique collection of struggles. Naively I thought people would automatically respect me if I were a minister. Because of my youthful appearance, that wasn't necessarily the case. One day Bonnie and I decided that I needed a reliable car I could use to visit my parishioners. So I decided to drop by the local car sales lot. I wandered through the lot until I found a solid looking Chevy. I kicked the tires, opened and shut the doors several times, and looked under the hood. When a salesman strolled by, I asked him if I could take it for a test drive.

He gave me the standard car-salesman grin. "Sure, Sonny, why don't you bring your dad down, and I'll let you take it out for a spin."

Bewildered, I shrugged my shoulders. "Uh, my dad doesn't live with me."

"What about your mom? Bring her down to test drive it with you."

By now it was a game for me. "She doesn't live with me either."

Exasperated, the man sputtered, "Well, who over twenty-one lives with you?"

"My wife."

"Come on. You can't be married yet!"

I could contain my grin no longer. "Oh, but I am married. And I'm twenty-five years old."

He shook his head. "Sorry, I don't buy that whopper either. I can't let you test drive any of our cars, Kid." I didn't buy a car that day, but I vowed that when I did, it wouldn't be from him.

By the end of my first year in Lewistown, I grew discouraged. Nothing seemed to be the way I'd expected it to be. One day I confided in a friend I'd made in the church. "Murray, I think I'm going to quit pastoring."

"Why?"

"Because pastoring isn't what I thought it would be."

"Tom, you can't quit."

"Why not?"

"Because whenever I attend your church I'm entertained."

I grimaced. "You're not supposed to be entertained."

"Oh, don't take it wrong. I didn't mean it that way. I mean I come to church feeling so-so and I leave feeling happy I was there. So you can't quit. Please don't quit."

* * *

My conference president insisted that I conduct a series of evangelistic meetings before I returned to the seminary for additional studies. I hadn't a clue as to how to put together twenty-one sermons for a series of meetings. Sure, I'd attended meetings, but write and present them myself?

Besides sermon preparation, I had another problem. In our small congregation, the only reliable musician, a pianist, was Carrie, a retired woman with a severe case of arthritis. When she played, if the audience didn't sing loud enough, she'd stop playing and scold everyone to sing louder before she would continue. How would visitors know she was really a loving, caring individual after such an outburst during the service?

I couldn't hurt Carrie by having someone else play "her piano." So to hold meetings I decided I would need an organist. I asked at a neighboring Christian church if the minister there knew of a good organist I might hire for the job. The pastor kindly gave me the name and address of their organist.

I drove to a home three blocks from our church and parked the car. *How lucky can I be?* I mused. *She could even walk to our church.* When I knocked on the door, I heard a commotion inside and the noise of pounding feet. The door swung open to reveal the smiling, eager faces of five girls between the ages of five and sixteen. Startled, I stuttered and stammered several half-attempts to explain myself. Finally I told them I was there to talk with their parents. They ushered me into their neatly arranged living room, where their parents, John and Rosanne, sat reading.

I smiled and introduced myself, hoping to have a private conversation with the parents. The five girls made themselves comfortable, eager to learn what I had to say.

After wringing my hands nervously, I stammered, "I'm holding a series of meetings at the church just down the street." I gestured in the correct direction. "And I was wondering if I could hire you to play the organ for me during the meetings?"

John's face hardened. "Absolutely not! I know what you're up to. You just want to convert my wife—and I won't have it!"

Stunned by his blustering, I tried to assure him that I just wanted to hire an organist. "Honest, Sir. I'm willing to pay. And you're welcome to come too, to make sure she doesn't make any decisions you wouldn't want her to make." I was really nervous now.

The girls switched their gaze from their father's angry face, to me, and then back again. I felt like a child again, ready to bolt for the door in a flash. The only thing that held my feet and my body in the room was my dire need for an organist and the threat of unemployment if I did not hold the meetings.

John muttered something under his breath, eyed me critically through the spectacles on the end of his nose, and pursed his lips. "OK, but no funny stuff! I'll be on the front row to make sure you don't pull a fast one." After a long pause, he flashed an order to his daughters. "And you, Girls, stay away from that church, you hear?"

I thanked him profusely and left. Relieved to escape, I hurried home to solve my next problem, twenty-one sermons that I borrowed from several evangelists I respected. On the first evening of the series, in addition to the church members, the organist and her husband were two of the half dozen visitors who attended.

Unbeknownst to their father, the girls pretended to go to bed before their mother and father left for the meetings. Once their parents left for church, they'd wait fifteen minutes, walk to the church, and peer in the back windows until their mother finished playing the last song and sat beside her husband. Then they would sneak in and sit in the back pew until their mother got up to play the last hymn, and then they'd slip out the back door and run home.

At the end of the three weeks, I made an altar call. John came forward. Standing in front of me, John said he was there for him and his wife as well. I looked up in time to see the girls coming down the center aisle. Although startled to see them, John was pleased that the entire family would be joining the church at the same time.

I'd survived my first series of evangelistic meetings. By the time I returned to the seminary the following summer, I felt much better about my pastoring skills. Before long I'd finished my stint at the seminary, and we headed west once more to Shelby, Montana, where we would pastor a three-church district that also included churches at Choteau and Havre.

While holding meetings in Havre, Montana, Bonnie and I arranged for a children's program to be conducted at the same time in the church basement. One week into the program one of the children broke out with chickenpox. Within days every child had the disease, including our two-year-old daughter, Kelly. Two-year-olds don't sleep well when they're uncomfortable. As a result, the parents of the two-year-old don't sleep well either.

One night Kelly wasn't settling down at all. It had been days since Bonnie had had a night of uninterrupted sleep. At two in the morning, I told Bonnie that I would take Kelly for a ride in the car, which always settled her down. "I'll take the dirty diapers along to the laundromat and kill two birds with one stone."

I had driven for no more than fifteen minutes when Kelly stopped fussing. By the time I arrived at the laundromat, she was sound asleep in the back seat. Leaving the car running, I dashed into the all-night laundromat and dumped the soiled diapers into a top-loading washing machine. I wasn't about to repeat history!

Once I was certain that the washer was functioning correctly, I climbed back into my car and drove slowly through town. It would be a long night. I passed a car sales lot and decided it would be a good time to check out their inventory without the presence of a pesky salesman. After touring the first lot, I went to two more. On my way to the fourth lot, flashing lights appeared in my rearview mirror. Puzzled, I glanced down at my speedometer. I was well under the limit.

I pulled over to the curb. Two strapping police officers strode up to my open window. The older man growled, "What do you think you're doing?"

Thinking there might be a town curfew, I explained that I was driving around town to get my sick daughter to sleep, and I'd stopped to wash a load of diapers at the laundromat.

"No, that's not what I want to know. What were you doing in the car lots?"

"Oh, I was just checking out their inventory. I hope to buy a new . . ."

"Open your trunk!"

"Sure." I hopped out of my car and obliged. "What are you looking for?"

"Hubcaps!" Satisfied that I had nothing in my trunk, the officers asked to see my driver's license. I reached into my pocket. It was empty. I'd left all my I.D. at home.

"I am so sorry. I guess in my haste to get my daughter to sleep, I forgot . . ."

"Where do you work?" the second officer asked.

"I'm a minister at the Seventh-day Ad . . ."

Two six-celled flashlights suddenly blinded me. "You expect us to believe that line?" One look at my disheveled hair and casual clothing, they burst out laughing.

"Yes, I do." By now I was certain I was going to jail. All I had to prove I was who I claimed to be was my sleeping daughter in the back seat. They peered at her pocked face and backed away from the car.

"OK, you can bring your driver's license to the police station at nine o'clock in the morning. And if you aren't there, we'll come looking for you."

The insecurities from my abusive childhood came back to haunt me when I entered the police station at nine o'clock the next morning and overheard the two officers laughing and bragging to the desk sergeant about how they scared some preacher in the middle of the night.

on the air

My insecurities went into overdrive when the Shelby church board decided that I should generate a fifteen- to twenty-minute program on a local fifty-thousand-watt radio station, KSEN. I wasn't too sure the idea was something I could or wanted to do, but always trying to please, I agreed to approach Jerry Black, the station manager, with their idea.

My knees knocked when I shook Mr. Black's hand and proposed that my church buy a fifteen- to twenty-minute time slot on his station.

His response was instant. Following a popular expletive, he snorted, "No way will I allow that to happen!"

In for a penny; in for a pound. I asked, "Why not?"

"Religious programming is the worst programming we have on the station! Nobody, but nobody listens to it. It is totally out of the question!"

A smile of relief swept across my face. *That's one project I won't get roped into doing against my will.* I rose to my feet, thanked Jerry for his time, and turned to leave his office.

"Wait a minute." He called me back. "I have an idea. It's never happened before, but if big corporations like Coca-Cola or General Motors can sell their product in sixty seconds, why can't preachers sell religion in the same amount of time?"

I shrugged my shoulders. "I don't know."

"If you come up with two weeks' worth of sixty-second spots, I'll sell you the time. For that matter I'll sell you any time you want."

I muttered all the way to the parking lot. "Lord, what have I gotten myself into this time? I can't do radio! I don't know the first thing about doing radio."

Two weeks later I returned to the station with two weeks' worth of sixty-second radio spots and a desired time slot. I remembered my proposal to Bonnie—why not go for broke? The worst that could happen would be for him to throw me out of his office. Would that be so bad? Then I wouldn't have to worry about writing any more spots.

He glanced through my notes and asked what time of day I wanted.

"Just before Paul Harvey in the morning and just before Paul Harvey at noon."

"You got it."

Now I was stuck! I'd imagined that stations kept those prime spots for their best customers. I would have the spot just before Paul Harvey. I was really nervous now!

For one year I talked about general topics, such as marriage, the family, healthful living, and news of what the Seventh-day Adventist Church was doing around the world. One day as I was recording my programs for the week, the manager strode into the studio.

"You know, this one-minute program of yours is doing OK, but we need to put a little pizzaz into the show."

"How is that?"

"You need to talk about some controversial issues, something that will make people sit up and think. Can you do that?"

"Sure can, but you might not like it." My mind had already leaped off the topic in my hand and was generating new possibilities. My first show under the new format, I talked about how unhealthful it is to eat pork. After recording two weeks' worth of scripts, I left for a short trip. When I came home, Bonnie met me at the door.

"Jerry Black of KSEN wants to speak with you. He said 'as soon as possible.' "

I hadn't a clue what he wanted. When I walked into his office, Jerry jumped up from his chair and gestured wildly. "Look what you've done to us!"

I was bewildered. He gestured toward a mountain of mail on a small table by his desk. "See this mail? Your program evoked so much fear about eating pork that we've been flooded with letters. Now the Montana Association of Hog Raisers is demanding equal time! Worse yet! We have to give it to them free! That's twenty minutes!"

I eyed the stacks of letters and swallowed hard. "Really? I'm sorry. I'll never do it again."

He snorted. "Like so much you will never do that again! I want you to come up with more controversial subjects. The people love it. This is the best publicity we've had in years!"

The next surprise was the Chamber of Commerce in Shelby asking whether I would serve as the chairman of the Medical Recruitment Committee. It was our job to attract medical talent to the community. As a result, the local hospital was totally restructured, and the number of town physicians tripled from one to three. Due to the sixty-second program and new members moving to our town, interest was sparked for building a private parochial school.

One day I drove past an abandoned golf course sitting high on a hill and overlooking the entire town. "What a great place that would be for a church school!"

On my way through town I stopped at the bank and asked who owned it.

"Dr. Stephen Aadaskovich."

"Could you tell me where he lives?"

The bank manager frowned. "You don't want to know."

"Why?"

"He's a very mean man. In fact, he got so mad at us, he pulled out his assets and put them in our competitor's bank. He's the largest land-owner in Toole County."

"Well, where does he live?" I was persistent.

"I'll tell you, but you shouldn't go out there alone. He has a vicious attack dog he'll let loose on you." The man shook his head to emphasize his point.

"I really want to see for myself." My desire to explore and find out things for myself often caused me more pain than I care to admit. I followed the directions to his home, pulled into the driveway, and climbed out of my car. Standing near the open car door, I glanced around for the infamous dog. I didn't see anything remotely danger-ous. I was halfway to the man's front door when I heard the growl.

A giant German shepherd whipped around the corner of the house, snarling and baring his teeth, acting like he could dismember me with one bite. With my pathway back to my car barred by the intimidating animal, I cautiously continued walking toward the house's front door. I knocked on the door. Nothing happened. I knocked again. By now the dog was circling me, as if trying to determine which thigh would produce the juiciest pre-dinner snack.

Just as the animal moved in for his kill, the door opened, and the man on the other side of the screen door grumbled, "Well I see you made it this far. What do you want?"

Difficult answer, I thought, staring at the raging canine. *Calling off your dog would be nice!*

Expecting to become dog food, I trembled. "I want to talk to you about your country-club property."

"What about it?"

By now I had to shout over the dog's bark. "We were wondering if we could rent it for a school?"

"No!"

"Why?"

"I don't want the liability!"

"Do you mind if I at least look at it?"

"Sure, look at it all you want, but that's all you can do."

I smiled at him. "Thanks. I think I will."

"Beg your pardon?" He leaned into the screen and cupped his ear.

Shouting over the dog's racket, I said, "Thank you. I think I will."

"Oh, shut up, you stupid mutt! Get in here and be quiet!" He opened the screen door and beckoned the animal inside. The dog hung his head and padded into the house. It could have been my imagination, but I was sure I saw a sheepish grin on the canine's face.

Driving up the gently winding road, I could see that the club house was definitely run down. I saw evidence of beer parties and spots where fires had been lighted and extinguished. As I drove back to Dr. A's, I planned my course of action.

"Sir," I began when Dr. A answered the door. This time his pooch was my slobbering buddy. "You know, our school would not be a liability to you, but that building is." I told him about the fires and the evidence of late-night parties. "If someone were to get hurt in there, you would be sued. Why don't you let us take it over? We'll pay for the liability insurance and renovate it at our expense if you will let us have it for five years."

For the first time, Dr. A sounded civil. "Two years!"

I shook my head. "Two years isn't enough. Five years."

"Three years."

"Five years." I held firm.

"Four."

I folded my hands across my chest. "We'd barely have gotten started in that amount of time."

"OK, you can have it for five years, rent free, as long as you do all the maintenance on it and fix it up."

I grinned and extended my hand. "You've got a deal!"

I wondered about the smirk that returned to his face as he shook my hand, what he might be holding back. But I quickly disregarded that thought.

The church members rejoiced. Finally we would have a Christian school. After signing the papers, the members of the church and I started cleaning up the place. We'd gotten quite a way into the project when someone suggested we ask the city to turn on the water.

"The six-inch water pipe going up to the building broke years ago," the city councilman informed me. "It will take ten thousand dollars to fix it."

"Ten thousand dollars?" I'd never seen that much money let alone been responsible for raising it.

"Yep! That's why the golf course was moved closer to the river—so they'd be closer to a water source. Dr. Aadaskovich knew that."

"So that's the reason for his smirk," I murmured under my breath. By now we'd spent a lot of time and bought a lot of material for the renovation. I exhaled slowly and trudged to my car. Where would our little congregation get ten thousand dollars to replace a water pipe? My shoulders slumped in discouragement as I climbed into my car. Somehow I had to tell my parishioners the bad news. Before I could start my engine, an old beat-up pickup drove up beside me. Dr. Aadaskovich leaned across the front seat of his car and rolled down his window. "What's the problem?"

I explained the problem to him.

"Oh, that's too bad," he said coldly. "It's your problem. Good luck." And he drove off.

That night I told my church board what the city council member had told me. We asked God for guidance in solving our water pipe situation. The next day the mayor called me. "What did you do to Dr. Aadaskovich?"

"I didn't do anything."

"Oh, yes you did."

"I did?"

"You come on down to my office. I need to talk with you."

"All right. I'll be right there." Reluctantly I drove to city hall. I had no idea what I might have done to insult the town's wealthiest curmudgeon. What if someone had killed him or something?

When I walked into his office, the mayor shook my hand enthusiastically. "I still want to know what you did to Dr. A."

"I really don't know what you're talking about. He was fine when he left me yesterday morning."

"Well, the doctor came into my office, plopped down a ten-thousand dollar check on my desk, and said, 'Fix that water line!' He's never been so generous to anyone in his entire life. The next time I need to negotiate with him, I'm sending you!"

I felt bemused by the strange turn of events. "Other than renovating the clubhouse into a school, I can't imagine what would possess him to support any church in the community!"

Dr. A grew more and more interested in what we were doing. Every day we worked on the building he was there telling us how to do things, assuring me that I needed a lesson in carpentry the Dr. A way. As old as he was, he knew how to dismantle things in a hurry and break them. By August we'd finished the renovations, and the school was ready to open. Bonnie was hired as the first teacher. High on the hillside, the school overlooked the entire town. It was an ideal location except during winter, when the wind swept through from the west and whipped around the building, dropping the inside temperatures so low the children had to stay bundled in lap blankets to keep warm. During warm-weather recesses the children got their exercise chasing prairie dogs into their holes.

* * *

Everywhere Bonnie and I went, we found kids in crisis. I tried to ignore God's obvious leading, but I couldn't. These children needed my help. I hated seeing others suffer through the same experiences I had as a child. So again, despite the birth of our first child, Kelly, Bonnie and I began spending time rescuing young people from bad circumstances and finding homes for them when theirs were not appropriate.

While living in Shelby, Montana, I became friends with a superior court judge. One day he suggested, "Tom, I think you would make a good juvenile probation officer. And if you don't mind, I'll write to my counterpart in Gallatin County and recommend you for the position they have open." I walked out of his office wondering what he knew about me that I didn't.

After four years in the Shelby district, the conference transferred us to the Ronan district, where I accomplished a lifelong dream: I learned to fly and purchased a World War II L-5 Stinson plane. I didn't realize it at the time, but this experience flying would become a blessing when God led us into a full-time ministry working with children.

The turning point for me in working with at-risk children came after we transferred to southern Oregon. By this time our son, Craig, had been born. A physician's family took us under their wing, helping us adjust to our new pastorate. Brian, their fifteen-year-old son, was having problems. I enjoyed taking their teenage son flying and hiking.

One night I got a call saying their son had been arrested for arson. Brian had attempted to burn down a drug store and a motel in the small community where he lived. Along with the arson charges, he was arrested for drug trafficking. Out of respect to the family, the judge sent him to a boys' ranch. He hadn't been there a week before he attempted to set fire to a field and a tractor.

That's when my friend called me for help. I listened quietly as the grieving father recited the events leading up to the moment. "Tom, they have Brian in detention. The judge is going to send my son to the McClaren School for Boys until he's twenty-one. Please, can you do something?"

"I really don't know, but I'll try. Who did you say is the judge on his case?"

The doctor told me, and I promised to do the best I could to keep the boy out of the system. When we hung up, I went to see the judge.

"Your Honor, can't we find any possible alternative to detention school for this young man?"

The judge gave me a wry smile. "Well, that's a good and noble thought, but the courts don't have the time, the energy, or the finances to do that."

I ran my hand distractedly through my hair. I had to come up with something. "Would you let him do something different from going to

McClaren if I found an alternative at no cost to the county or the state?" I didn't have a clue where this would lead.

"Yes, if the place follows a rigid criteria." He proceeded to spell out the ten conditions one at a time. One of the conditions was that the boy was to live as far away from a populated area as possible yet close enough to report for psychiatric counseling every week. Another was that the couple who took him in had to have college degrees.

When I snorted and told him that I thought that rule was ridiculous, the judge reminded me that he was the judge and if I wanted to do something for this boy, I would follow his orders to the letter. As the judge spelled out the criteria, an idea grew in my mind. Montana! God had placed me in Montana where I met a family who would meet all ten of the judge's conditions perfectly. But would they agree to my scheme?

Several phone calls and less than a week later, Brian and his mother were flying with me to Montana. Within a year and a half, he had improved so dramatically that the judge released him from probation, freeing him to go wherever he wished. Brian finished his schooling and returned home to live a very responsible life.

When the word got out that I had helped the boy, other people called, asking for help to save their children as well. Between pastoring and helping parents with their at-risk children, I had little time for my own family.

One night I arrived home at suppertime and found Bonnie sick in bed.

"Tom, would you please fix supper for the kids?"

A simple enough request. "Sure, Honey."

Not being a very good cook, I figured I'd fry up a pan of potatoes and scrambled eggs—the only meal I knew how to make. Making my way to the kitchen, I had sliced the potatoes and removed the frying pan from the cupboard when the phone rang. It was one of my parishioners.

"Pastor, we need to see you immediately."

I looked first at the frying pan and then at the stack of sliced potatoes on the cutting board. "Sure, I'll be right over." I wiped my hands on a hand towel and strode to the base of the stairs and called, "Bonnie, I've got to go. Someone needs me."

I grabbed my coat and headed toward the door, where I found Bonnie, weak and pale, leaning against the doorframe. "Is it possible that someday the kids and I could get an appointment with you?"

Her words smacked me right between the eyes. Without hesitation I went to the phone and called the people I'd arranged to see. "I'm really sorry. I'll have to meet with you tomorrow. My wife isn't feeling well, and the kids need me to fix supper."

They were very understanding. They assured me that our meeting could wait a couple of days. *Wait a minute,* I thought. *Five minutes ago our meeting was urgent; now it can wait a couple of days.*

Not long after I was at a pastors' meeting where the guest speaker said, "Every ten years a minister needs to reflect on where he is, where he's been, and where he wants to be." It struck me that I had been exactly ten years in the ministry, and somehow I was neglecting my family to take care of other people's families. Something had to change. I hadn't married Bonnie to relegate her to the position of nanny and chief cook and bottle washer. Where had I lost sight of the fact that I married her because I loved her and enjoyed spending time with her? More important, I still did. Obviously, I needed to make a few priority adjustments in my life.

out the gate

"A leave of absence?" My friend was baffled. "People will think you did something wrong and were forced to leave the ministry!"

"Probably so, but Bonnie and I have talked it over. We need time to refocus on our family. I've been too busy, and my children are growing up without me. I don't want that to happen."

"But pastors aren't supposed to take leaves of absence!"

I knew my friend meant well, but so did I. "Maybe more should."

Living on eighty acres, in a house not visible from the road, allowed us the luxury of disappearing from view. Even though we had a gate at the entrance to our property, for the first week or two, I left it ajar, thinking that I, as a pastor, had little right to privacy.

Early one morning a visitor drove up our driveway, got out of his car and, after a short greeting, began complaining about the pastor who had replaced me. After he finished his litany of complaints and I reminded him that I was no longer the one to whom he should speak regarding his problems, we parted as friends. I followed him down the driveway and locked the gate behind him, opening it only rarely for the next three months. I refused to allow myself to be drawn into the local church politics, issues, or what people thought of their new pastor. I would play with my children and get reacquainted with my wife. It was wonderful. For three months Kelly, Craig, Bonnie, and I spent wonderful time together. I even built my daughter a one hundred-square-foot tree house and my son, Craig, a fort, complete with a guard tower. In between building projects, we searched for an elusive gold stash folklore claimed was hidden along the banks of Hog Creek, which ran through our property.

At the end of three months the conference president called. "It's time for you to get back to work. We have a church waiting for you at Hood River. Please come."

The news that we had created alternatives to detention in southern Oregon followed us to Hood River. Little did Bonnie or I comprehend how our move to Hood River would impact the direction our lives of service would take. People from all over the state called. "If you could do what you did for Brian, would you be willing to do the same for my son or my daughter?" When we provided alternatives or special foster placements for a couple of child-abuse cases, the news spread.

One of the defining moments came when Sarah, a fifteen-year-old who had attempted to burn down a church and had attempted suicide, came into our lives. After spending a couple of nights in detention, her juvenile probation officer called me. "I understand that you have a history of providing detention for young people. We'd like to see what you can do with this young lady."

I listened as the officer explained Sarah's problem. "She's not talking. And we don't feel she needs detention. What she does need is to be far away from her family dynamics in order to determine what is really going on."

Before the probation officer hung up, I agreed to look for a place. I told him I'd get back to him. I called my friends in Montana. They agreed to provide a place where Sarah could begin to heal. I phoned the probation officer back. "I'll be willing and happy to help Sarah make the transition to Montana."

"Well, you fly. Why don't you fly her there?" The officer was right, I did have my pilot's license. However, I no longer had an airplane.

I cleared my throat. "Well, because I don't have any money."

"Tell you what. We'll pay for the trip up until you cross the border from Oregon into Idaho. Then you'll have to find a way to pay for the rest."

I quickly contacted the local Adventist Community Services center. They knew the girl and agreed to come up with the balance of the money as well as enough funds to rent an aircraft in which Sarah and I could fly to eastern Montana.

With the money raised, I contacted the probation officer. "Hey, I need a chaperone."

"Hmm, I've never seen eastern Montana, and I have some time off coming to me," the probation officer declared. "Would I pass for an escort?"

"Sure, why not?"

What an adventure! We landed in a bumpy cow pasture close to the ranch house.

* * *

Soon after this experience a judge in the state of Oregon declared that no juvenile could be housed in the same building as an adult criminal. This ruling prohibited using most current detention facilities for juvenile offenders. The state then established a juvenile services commission for each county in the state. The local commission invited me to help research and write a grant proposal to provide alternatives to placing underage children in criminal detention facilities.

The Hood River County commissioners voted to require a home setting for any juvenile who was arrested until the child was taken to court. The Next Door, Inc., a residential program for teenage boys, was awarded the grant, and I was asked to serve on the subcommittee to research the location of possible homes.

The director and I were talking one day about the program. "Would your wife be interested in taking in juveniles who are under house arrest? It's a good opportunity and pays for simply being on call and more if there is a child in the home."

"I don't know what Bonnie would think about that. But it wouldn't hurt to ask her."

"Why don't you call her and ask her to come in?"

I called Bonnie immediately, not having a clue how she'd feel about such a proposition. Within a short time she appeared at the director's office.

Patiently she listened to the director's proposal. "So what do you think?"

"Absolutely not!"

"Why?" The director didn't become director for lack of persistence.

"Number one, our children are five and ten years old. Second, I believe I should be the one in my home choosing what my children watch on TV. Third, we eat a low-fat and low-sugar vegetarian diet."

The director rolled his chair back from his desk, leaned back, and clasped his hands behind his neck. "You know, that sounds just exactly like what we need."

Bonnie shook her head vigorously. "You don't understand. The children won't like it there."

But the director wasn't listening. Instead, he was riffling through his desk files. Pulling out a document, he plopped it on his desk. "The state of Massachusetts is doing a similar program with dramatic results. The kids aren't allowed to watch TV or read comics. And they are put on a strict diet—no junk food. The success rate has been measured in a matter of months for these kids."

After much persuasion Bonnie relented with the provision that she have a back-up family. "I can't be on call twenty-four hours a day, seven days a week without some sort of relief."

"Fine. You find a family you would like to work with, and we will do the same for them." We chose Donna and Walt Shelman as our "back-up" couple. They supplied a great relief every two weeks.

The initial program became known as JAM—Jail Alternative Measure. The Next Door, Inc., outfitted every door in our house with alarms and secured many of our windows as well. Before we could begin taking in other people's children, we needed to involve our own children in the project. We offered to pay them every night that they had to vacate their beds and "camp out" in our bedroom. The nights we had teenagers in the house became a treat for our kids. The thirty to forty dollars a month proved to be a powerful motivator. A few months into the program, there was a lapse in the number of children staying with us and Craig asked, "Can't you get some kids into our house pretty soon?"

I asked him why, and he replied, "I need some money!"

As you might imagine, life was not always blissful when dealing with troubled children. One afternoon we had three girls staying with us under house arrest who'd run away from their homes. They'd been chatting in the living room with Bonnie when Bonnie excused herself for a brief moment to go to the bathroom. Before she returned, they'd bolted out the door and down the hill.

Immediately Bonnie called me at work. Then she called the police, the boy's home director, and CSD—Children's Services Division. By the time I got home, the state police were there. One of the officers and I started off across a field near our house, searching for them, when I spotted them in the woods.

"There they are!" I pointed and started running in the direction of our runaways. The policeman soon passed me. Catching up to them in no time, he whipped out two sets of handcuffs and radioed for another set. Once he had them restrained, he turned to me. "Tom, I can take only two in my patrol car, so you will have to walk this one back to your house by yourself."

He handcuffed her to me, and we walked the three quarters of a mile back to my house. Walking and holding hands is not very restrictive, but walking handcuffed to another person is torture. It's sort of like bull-riding when you have your hand secure in the cinch and you want to get loose, but you can't. The twisting and turning causes the metal cuff to scrape the skin off your wrist with every effort your prisoner makes to break free.

My pace quickened as my discomfort intensified. I wanted to get her home before she injured us both any further. She quit fussing only when we had her secure on our sofa with Bonnie on one side and me, handcuffed to her, on the other. Two hours passed. Desperate to be free of her, I asked Bonnie to call the police and ask a police officer to come and unlock the cuffs.

* * *

"Bonnie, I'm heading out for prayer meeting. Is there anything you need while I'm in town?" I grabbed my car keys and headed toward the kitchen door.

"No, but thanks for asking." She and the kids were washing the last of the supper dishes.

Ring! I glanced toward Bonnie and heaved a sigh. I'd almost made it out the door. "I hope this doesn't take long. I'll be late for sure." It rang a second time. Being nearest to the jangling phone, I answered it.

"Mr. Sanford, this is the sheriff's department. We have a juvenile here that you need to pick up."

"Hold on. This is my wife's job, not mine." I covered the mouthpiece. "Bonnie, it's the sheriff's department. They have a kid for you to pick up."

She began shaking her head before I finished speaking. "Tell them we can't do that. We already have two others here."

I removed my hand from the mouth piece. "My wife says she can't take another one right now."

"Look, we're short staffed here. You have to take him."

"Hold on, please." I covered the mouthpiece again. "Bonnie, he says we have to. They're short staffed." I could see her resistance weakening. "The courthouse is right on my way to the church. I'll be glad to pick him up for you."

She threw up her hands in surrender.

"Sheriff, I'll be there for the boy in fifteen minutes." I hurried out the door before Bonnie could change her mind.

At the courthouse I introduced myself and told them I was there for the boy. The desk sergeant gestured toward a cocky, slovenly dressed young man with his shirt unbuttoned and wide open. The room was filled with his curses at the police for picking him up. I strode over to where they had him handcuffed and introduced myself.

"I want you to know that this is not my job. This is my wife's job, but she couldn't come down to pick you up this evening. So since I'm on my way to my regular job, I agreed to take you along." I eyed him through my laid-back, easy going demeanor. "I'm a minister, and right now, I have to go to the church and conduct prayer meeting. You're welcome to go with me, but you don't have to. It's your choice."

The boy blinked. "I haven't been to church since I was a little kid, and I'm not going to start now."

I shrugged. "Fine, you don't have to go." I turned to leave.

"What will happen to me while you're at prayer meeting?"

"They'll keep you right here in the sheriff's office until I come back."

It didn't take the young man long to decide he'd rather come with me than to stay handcuffed in the sheriff's office the rest of the evening. "What do I have to do to get ready for prayer meeting?"

I nodded toward his unbuttoned shirt. "Button up completely and tuck it in. Then you'll be OK for prayer meeting."

His fingers couldn't have moved faster. He couldn't have been more cooperative. He turned out to be one of the nicest young men we ever had in our home.

One young runaway staying with us told Bonnie she wanted to learn a hobby. Bonnie started her on a craft and left the room only to return to find that the girl had cut the screen and crawled out. The window alarm would have sounded if she'd pushed the screen instead of cutting it. We immediately called the police, who called us back a couple of hours later. "It's so amazing. She ran away from you and ran right back to her home. She vowed she'd never run away again. So the problem we thought that would be solved only in court was very easily accomplished."

Within a year I was asked to serve as the chairman of Juvenile Services Commission. Our committee worked on various projects to get money from the state of Oregon to create alternatives or assistance in keeping juveniles out of state detention facilities. I was soon discouraged. With all the time and effort fifteen or sixteen volunteers put into writing plans and programs then getting only two thousand or three thousand dollars back to assist seemed to be wasted effort.

I was almost asleep one night when Bonnie shook my shoulder. "Tom, I've been thinking: We're spending an awful lot of time providing temporary fixes for these kids, and then they're gone. Why don't we do this full time? Why don't we try to help teenagers on a long-term basis rather than just the overnighters?"

"Yeah, Honey. Good idea." I rolled over and snuggled down to sleep once more.

"No, no! I'm serious. Why don't you start a program of your own to help at-risk kids?"

"I'll look into it, Honey." I knew she was right. There were a number of young people from the churches I'd pastored who were in trouble. Maybe I should begin with my own church.

The next morning Bonnie and I discussed the idea further. She was as excited as I was about the possibilities. "We could explore the possibilities with our pastors and find out just what the need might be."

After breakfast I drove into Portland to our conference president's office. I was ushered in with a friendly greeting and handshake. We chatted about the weather and about activities of my own congregation. "Sir, I'm here with a proposition. As you know, at-risk teens are a burden on my heart."

He nodded graciously. "Yes, and we appreciate all that you're doing in your local community."

"Well, this is my idea." I told him about our desire to create a service for our own Seventh-day Adventist young people and their parents. "What do you think?"

He shook his head condescendingly. "There's no way something like that would work within our church. There's no problem with our young people. The worst problems our kids have is smoking behind the barn or making out with a girl behind the dormitory—but nothing more serious than that."

His answer caught me by surprise. Had I been looking at this all wrong? Was I so close to these troubled young people coming through my home that I'd begun to see all teens as being at risk when only a few really were?

Unnerved, I talked with another conference administrator. I explained my concerns and my plan. His reply was simple and to the point. "Personally, I think we should disfellowship kids caught violating the standards of the church. And when they get their act together, we can accept them back into the congregation!"

I blinked in surprise. "Aren't you worried that with that kind of thinking they might never come back to the church? People tend to return to the last place they felt love. You can't feel love in a place where you were disfellowshipped."

"Hmm." He thought for a moment. "I see your point. Maybe I should reevaluate my position."

I agreed with him that a reevaluation of his position might be a good idea. I talked with other administrators. Their opinions varied according to their position in the organization. Some felt that it was too big of a project, and the church wasn't ready or willing to get involved in what they saw as a "social welfare program."

By the time I drove home, I was discouraged. I could see no hope for this plan He'd given me. I told Bonnie about the negative responses our idea received.

"You can't quit" was Bonnie's reply. "Why would God pay us to be trained and not use us for His service?"

from a tiny seed ...

"Tom, if you really want to find out if you are the only one dealing with these situations, why don't you survey the pastors in the conference? You could do it through my office. That way we can see how extensive a problem it really is." Charles Dart, the educational superintendent, leaned back in his chair. An encouraging smile lit his face. Elder Dart had been an academy principal. If anyone had dealt with at-risk teenagers, this man had. He had worked with Sarah and knew that somewhere in her short life there was a dark secret she wasn't revealing to anyone.

His suggestion made sense to me. I'd make up a little questionnaire and send it to the approximately 100 pastors who pastored the 150 congregations in the Oregon Conference. The results of the survey told us that in one year's time, 150 young people from those congregations needed out-of-home placement. Because they had few options, many of these children were randomly placed in foster homes by Children's Service Division. Were the youth of Oregon unique, or was this a problem common to other conferences in the North Pacific Union?

I presented my findings to the leaders of the North Pacific Union. Again, they said this was something way over their heads. The union conference president, Richard Fearing, invited me to present my findings to the conference presidents. "For that matter, presidents of the Montana, Idaho, Upper Columbia, Washington, Oregon, and Alaska conferences are meeting next week at Sun River. Why don't you come down and share your concerns right after lunch on Wednesday?"

It proved to be a great lunch. Many of the attendees were dozing off. Others were doodling while I presented my proposal. Elder Theodore Carcich, a saintly old man and former church leader who had been invited to present the meeting's devotionals, noticed that not many people were paying attention to my presentation. Suddenly he lifted his hand in the air.

I noticed that the higher his hand raised, the tighter his fist became—when all at once he slammed it down on the table top. Everyone was startled awake and stared at him. "Brethren, I support a Catholic priest in New York City who takes care of his own. The minute the Adventist Church takes care of its own, I will support that program as well!"

His pronouncement switched the afternoon topic from a why-should-we proposal to a how-can-we-implement-such-a-program discussion.

A finance official weighed in. "The fact is that, unfortunately, there is not enough money in the budget to add another program."

One of the union-conference people said, "There might be if the local conferences do away with some of their more frivolous programs."

"Frivolous!" A local-conference representative leaped to his feet. "No! No! No! The local conference has no frivolous programs, but the union conference certainly has a few."

A brief disagreement ensued until both concluded that neither had funds in their budget to support a new program. Both the local-conference and union-conference representatives finally agreed that the only way my proposal could be implemented would be if it was a self-funding program supported through donations.

Between the afternoon meetings, Elder Fearing confided to me, "You know, I think that the best thing that could happen to this new program would be for it to survive on its own. If it becomes just another department, every time you needed money to support a child or to move a youngster or to provide resources for a child, you'd have to go through a committee. And sometimes, you're not going to have the time to go through such a committee."

When the meeting resumed, the conference officers discussed how to raise the start-up money for the program. They determined that it would take thirty-nine thousand dollars for one year of operation. Dr. Howard Ferguson, who had attended to lend support to my proposal, raised his hand. "I will be the first to give one thousand dollars. But I want my money back if you don't allow this program to start. And if you do, then the money will be well spent."

The union committee decided to include three articles in the *Gleaner*, the North Pacific Union church paper, to see what kind of financial support would be available. They also offered to give me a one-year leave of absence from pastoring. During that time I would be totally dependent on donations to get the program started. They also declared that the program wouldn't start until we had the full thirty-nine thousand dollars in hand.

I sang all the way back to Hood River. Grinning from ear to ear, I announced the good news to my family. "The first thing we need is a name and a logo for the program." Even as I told them what had happened, I wondered, *Why am I so happy? This project is going to be a lot of work, an uphill climb all the way.* Yet as I looked around the table at the faces of my wife and children who also felt it was a good idea, I realized why I was so happy. I had a family rallying behind me and pushing me forward.

"I don't see the problem." Bonnie's eyes glistened with the same enthusiasm I recognized the first time we met. "I realize that our family finances will be dramatically at risk during the next twelve months, but I think we should proceed anyway. God has led us this far. We need to trust Him to provide."

Our daughter Kelly sketched out the logo that we've used since the beginning in 1984. From that concept, we developed the acronym PATCH—Planned Assistance for Troubled Children. A board of directors was established, with Sam Lefore of Milton-Freewater as the first chairman in 1983.

The *Gleaner* articles appeared in the October, November, and December issues. They told of this new program called Project PATCH that provided alternatives to young people needing out-of-home placement. Those three articles generated fifteen hundred dollars in donations along with pledges totaling five hundred dollars a month—nowhere near the thirty-nine thousand dollars we needed to begin the project.

On the first of January, I visited one of the union-conference leader's offices. I told him of our dilemma. We were receiving dozens of calls from parents who wanted us to find alternative placements for their teenagers some way or other. "What should I do?"

The leader shook his head and told me that the program would be cancelled if we didn't have the thirty-nine thousand dollars we'd expected to receive by January.

"Wait! You can't call it quits!" I was frantic. I'd been listening to all the heart-wrenching stories from desperate families around the state. I now realized we were seeing only the tip of the iceberg. How many children were out there whose parents hadn't read the articles? Worse yet, how many children were out there whose parents were abusing them and didn't want anyone to know about it? My own childhood flashed through my mind; I remembered praying that someone would rescue me from the physical beatings and verbal abuse. I had to help these kids, but what could I do? Their fate was in the hands of the people sitting before me.

"Well, maybe you can't, but we can." The administrator's voice shoved through my barrage of memories, jolting me back to the present.

"No, please, give me more time." I was ready to beg on my knees if necessary. The administrators looked at one another. One tapped his pen purposefully on the sheet outlining PATCH's financial report. Finally one of the men spoke.

"OK, we can give you until February fifteen to come up with the money. If the money isn't available by then, we'll call it quits."

After much prayer, I set out to solicit the funds myself. A friend of mine who had a heart for at-risk kids agreed to donate a thousand dollars a month to get it started. Another person donated ten thousand dollars. Together with the fifteen hundred dollars raised through the articles, we were close to the amount needed. I went back to the union administrator and told him about the money I'd raised.

"Who promised you the pledge of one thousand dollars a month?"

I told him.

He shook his head. "That person is unreliable. You can't depend on him at all."

Desperate and stubborn, I couldn't contain myself. "No, no, no, I don't believe that for a moment!"

We argued for some time. Finally he spoke, "OK. But remember, it's your family and it's your finances. If you're crazy enough to start something that is going to put your family at risk . . ."

"I just can't believe that the Lord is going to let us starve while we try to serve Him. He's the One who did miracles in our lives and led us by His Spirit." Amazingly, I felt a determination to stand up to my directors and say, "This is God's will; therefore, it's God's bill. I'll take the risk!"

The realization that I was not in control of anything was a little scary. I even received calls from friends who were concerned about the risk I was taking. For the first time, I felt totally dependant on God for everything that happened.

By this time Bonnie had burned out being a primary home for the jail-alternative program. So together we launched into the PATCH program full time. We rented an office suite in Hood River, Oregon. After the first year, when it appeared Project PATCH was not going away, we were invited to move to the conference headquarters in

Clackamas, Oregon. Scores of parents and other concerned family members were calling and asking for assistance. One family had a son named Aaron who was constantly getting into trouble at home. His parents begged us to find a place for him. "If you can't find a place, he's either going to end up in detention or jail!" We agreed to find a home for Aaron.

The day before we transferred Aaron to his new home, his parents brought him to our place in Hood River. As I helped him settle in for the night, I tried to assure him, "Don't worry, Aaron. This is only for tonight. Tomorrow you'll be heading for your new home."

"Where's that going to be?" The worried frown on his face deepened.

"We found you a great place in western Montana. You're going to love it there."

He looked skeptical. The next morning before we got ready to leave, I spotted him walking down the street. I ran to catch up with him. "What's wrong, Aaron? Where are you going?"

"I'm running away. You're not going to take me anywhere. I want to go home!" he cried. By this time Aaron was begging and pleading with me to let him go home.

"But your parents have already returned home. They're not here anymore."

"I want to go home! I'm not going with you. I want to run away."

My heart ached for him, but I had to be in control of the situation. "Look, Aaron, if you just keep on running down the hill, I'll have to call the police."

He thought about my threat for a minute. "OK, I'll go with you even if it kills me!"

I laughed. "It's not going to kill you." I tried to convince him that his life at the Wernick's Montana home would be nowhere near as dangerous as the one he'd been leading at home.

Back at the house, I called Wayne Baer, a friend of mine in Ronan, Montana, and asked if he'd be willing to help transport this young man. He had helped me get my pilot's license, and I knew he would help me any way he could. I need you to fly us from Ronan to Polebridge. I want to get this kid settled as soon as possible. He's getting more and more antsy by the minute."

"I'd be happy to, Tom."

After a long, exhausting drive with Aaron as determined to go back home as I was to get him to where he needed to go, we arrived at Wayne's private airstrip in Ronan.

Wayne's Cessna 206 flew over the beautiful Flathead Valley and up the west side of Glacier National Park. Overwhelmed by the beauty below, I gazed out of the right side of the plane at the Mission Mountain Range and at the beautiful Flathead Lake on the left. As Flathead Lake disappeared behind us, I looked at Aaron. By the frown on his face, I knew he wasn't appreciating the beauty below. The lake narrowed to a winding river through a dense forest until the spectacular, high mountains of Glacier National Park came into view.

Aaron's expression didn't soften when we passed Lake McDonald, nor at the site of miles and miles of dense forest. Almost as if on cue, the dense foliage parted to reveal a narrow ribbon of an airstrip. As we climbed out of the plane, I turned toward Aaron. "Son, the only way out of here is up—and we're leaving. So you're going to have to grow wings if you're going to get out of here."

He looked up at the deep blue sky over our heads and at the tall corridor of evergreen trees. With a plaintive cry of a trapped animal, he said, "Oh, Lord, You're going to have to help me."

The Wernicks met Aaron at the airstrip and took him back to their home, the closest place on this earth to a Shangri-la if there ever was one. Everything went well for the first week until Linda Wernick broke her neck in a car accident, cutting short the experiences Aaron would have had there. However, a week was long enough for him to discover that there was another side of life. He learned to value some of his own family's experiences. He also learned that if he needed to use a telephone there, he had to walk five miles. He got a lot of exercise that week. Along the way, he managed to confront a bear as well.

* * *

Don, a young man in his early teens, had a history of shoplifting. He got into serious trouble with the law and was thrown into detention. Because Don had been living with his grandmother, his juvenile officer called and asked me if I had an alternative to detention for this young man.

"Perhaps. But before I start to look, can you tell me what interests this young man has, what he's done before that he might enjoy doing again, or what he's never done but can see himself doing?"

"Why do you need to know that stuff?"

"You've already told me what's wrong with him. Now I'd like to know his assets, some things about him on which we can build. He knows how bad he's been; I'll bet he needs to feel better about himself."

The man was silent for a moment. "I'll get the information for you, but I don't think it will do any good."

"Leave it to me. You get me the answers to my questions, and I'll be happy to consider the options after that."

A couple of days later, the officer called back. "Don says he's always wanted to fly an airplane. He would think he'd died and gone to heaven if he could learn to fly."

Again I called Wayne and Ruby Baer in Ronan, Montana. "Would you be willing to take a boy this time?" I explained about Don's history and his interest in learning to fly.

"Sure!" They took him into their home and into their hearts. By the time Don turned fifteen, he was doing so well that the state of Montana decided that it did not need to pay foster care for him any longer.

When asked the reason for the cessation of funds, the government official said, "The state can't do this."

Wayne contacted me and I contacted the juvenile officer in charge of Don's file. "If this young man were still an offender or shoplifting or into burglary or something, you'd continue to pay foster care. But because he is successful and has straightened out his life, you aren't going to help out?"

"You really have a passion for this, don't you?"

"Yes! We're not going to put all this effort into helping this young man only to discover that the state is going to sabotage it by destroying the foster placement!"

After I went through the necessary channels, the county court sued the state of Montana, and the Baers continued to receive foster payments for Don until his eighteenth birthday. As a result, Don stayed in the area and became a successful citizen of the community.

Summer months were especially difficult months to find homes for kids until I met Jeaneou and Judy Poirot. Jeaneou, an experienced mountain climber, had a Ph.D. in outdoor recreation. The couple heard about PATCH's need for summertime placement for children. "Wouldn't it be exciting to take a group of kids mountain climbing? If only we had a place where we could teach them some high and low rope climbing."

"A place? You'd do it if you had a place?" My mind was immediately turning. I contacted Fred and Velma Beavon, friends of mine who'd promised that they'd lend us their place near Whitehall, Montana, if we ever needed it. I called and explained our plan and asked if they would let us use their property for an entire summer. They agreed.

We sent half a dozen teens and preteens to live with the Poirots for the summer. With the Poirots' oldest daughter and a young man named Scott Byers to help, they spent the summer helping kids overcome personal fears and gain self-confidence in themselves through climbing and other outdoor activities. Thus began our summer program.

for such a time

"Have you noticed how down Albert has been lately?" Bonnie had wandered into my office while I was browsing through the classified ads for small airplanes. One in particular had caught my attention, a prototype of the Cessna 172.

"What about Albert?" Albert was one of my church members. It was unusual to see him depressed for such a long period of time.

I eyed the photo critically. It was a prototype because it was painted a different color than the regular Cessna 172 and had a three-blade propeller instead of the customary two-blade prop. If I wanted to see the plane in person, I would need to go to Kansas. "You know how I've been considering getting a plane—what with all the air travel I do for PATCH. I wonder if Albert would like to go with me to Kansas to check out this model?"

Bonnie collected the papers for which she'd come into my office. "A good idea. Why don't you ask him?"

I did. And Albert refused.

"But, Albert, you need to go with me." He refused again and again and again. By this point, I was convinced that the only way my friend would shake his heavy mood was to go with me on this reconnaissance mission. In desperation I spoke with his wife, Madaline. "What can I do to convince your hubby to go with me?"

A devilish grin spread across her face. "Buy his ticket and tell him he has to go."

Taking Madaline's advice, I bought Albert's ticket. I found him pruning his fruit trees in Mosier, Oregon. Not waiting for argument, I thrust the ticket into his hands. "Albert, I have a plane ticket to Kansas for you. We must leave Hood River at noon to catch the commercial flight at Portland."

Albert scowled at the ticket folder in his hands. "I told you I wasn't going to go!"

"I know, but I didn't believe you. I think you really ought to go."

Albert stared at the ticket for several seconds. "OK, I'll go."

"Good!"

Picking up the ladder, he headed for his truck. "I'll meet you back at my house."

When I drove up to his home, Madaline met me at the door. "You know what Albert said when he came into the house? He said, 'You got your way after all.' I told him that I didn't know it was my way, though I've been praying he'd go with you. He's been so discouraged."

We flew to Kansas, and the next morning, we purchased the plane. We headed west in the cold, clear blue February skies. As we flew over the Rockies, Albert turned to me and said, "You know, I've seen more country today than I've seen in my entire life. This is great."

Later that afternoon, we landed in Butte, Montana, to refuel. Leaving Butte, we flew over the Bitterroot Mountains near sunset. As it grew darker, I noticed that my amp meter registered in the negative and that my lights were dimming. I decided to turn off all lights except for the little light on my magnetic compass. Albert watched without saying a word as I followed the compass reading west toward Lewiston, Idaho.

As we approached the airport, I spotted another plane descending, and then another and another. I followed the planes until I saw the colored lights of the runway. I had to open the cockpit door after my wheels touched down so as not to stray off the taxiway or damage any of the airport's landing lights. When we rolled to a stop, I realized that none of the blue lights along the taxiway were lit. The taxiway on which I'd turned was not in use. When I called the tower after parking and told them I'd landed, they didn't believe me.

I chuckled. "I assure you that I am here in Lewiston, Idaho, and I need a mechanic."

They told me where I could get the plane repaired the next morning. Albert and I found a motel for the night and the next morning headed for the closest restaurant.

When Albert's breakfast arrived, a scoop of butter sat in the middle of his pancakes. "Ah, finally I get some ice cream. Madaline won't let me have ice cream at home." He beamed with delight.

I looked at him, then at the melting butter. " No, Albert, that's not ice cream. That's butter."

"Tom, I know ice cream when I see it!"

"It's butter."

"I'll prove it to you." Taking his spoon and scooping up the chunk of butter into his mouth, he stopped, blinked, and spit it out. With a sheepish grin, he said, "That's butter all right."

After getting the alternator repaired, we flew home without mishap.

Nine months later a note at the bank was due. So I sold the Cessna 172 for enough money to pay off the note, the interest, and the cost of the insurance. Albert didn't say much, but a few months later, he admitted that he was disappointed that I'd sold the plane. "Why did you sell it?" he asked.

"Well, I'm not sure of our month-to-month income, so I have to be very cautious with our finances."

"But you need the plane, especially now that you are transporting kids from place to place full time."

I shrugged. "I can't afford it, Albert."

"Why don't you do the same thing you did before—just borrow the money?"

"I can't take the risk of not being able to pay it back right now."

He let the topic drop for the short time, but then came back and asked me about the airplane. "You really do need an airplane. Tell you what, I'll loan you the money."

I shook my head. "I don't want to borrow the money."

"Then I'll loan PATCH the money."

"Thanks Albert, but no thanks. You're a good friend."

He leaned across my desk. "Look, sometimes my stock broker invests my money in places I don't know anything about, and if my wife ever finds out we have that stock in Caesar's World, she's going to throw a fit!"

I didn't know anything about Caesar's World, but I was certain his wife would indeed not like it.

Albert proceeded to tell me that if the stock went up to $18.50 a share, he would give PATCH the difference between $15.00 and $18.50 a share so that we could buy an airplane.

"No, Albert!"

The man was determined. "I'm going to do what I think is best. And I won't take No for an answer!"

A week later as my wife and I knelt beside our bed for our evening prayers, I said, "Maybe we should think about Albert's offer. PATCH really does need a plane of some kind."

We'd barely begun to pray when the telephone rang. It was Albert's daughter and son-in-law. We talked for some time about a child they'd taken into their home. Before I could say goodbye, Albert's daughter mentioned that her father was visiting them and wanted to speak with me.

"Tom?" He said in his gruffest voice, the one he used to intimidate people. "You been praying lately?"

"As a matter of fact, I have."

"You must have." He chortled.

"Why is that?"

"My stock went up to eighteen-fifty a share for a half an hour today, and I unloaded it. I have fifteen thousand dollars for you to buy a plane. So buy a plane!"

A week had passed when Albert barreled into my office once more.

"Madaline is on her way in here. I want to do all the talking. Don't you say anything."

I nodded in agreement, thinking he must be feeling guilty for investing his money in what we both had assumed was a questionable place of entertainment. When his wife entered my office, I greeted her, offered her a chair, and sat down to watch the show. Albert crossed his arms, acting very stern. He turned toward his wife. "Write PATCH out a check for fifteen thousand dollars and don't argue with me!"

A grin spread across her face. "Well, it's about time you did something decent with your money!" Through our exchanged smiles, I realized she'd known his little secret all along.

Thanks to Albert and Madaline's generosity, I purchased a used Cessna 182. And in less than five years, we logged eight hundred hours on that plane, transporting children from their homes to PATCH-approved foster homes. When FlightCraft at Portland International Airport learned about Project PATCH, they donated free hanger space and rolled out the red-carpet treatment each time we transported children to their new homes.

Many times parents would drop their child at our office and announce, "I don't ever want to see my kid again!"

The poor child would often be stunned and respond with, "But, Mom, what did I do to you?" The horrendous trauma of abandonment would ease somewhat when they learned we were taking them to the airport where they would be treated so well. Bonnie, as the chaperone, would give them the motherly care they needed to soothe their fears.

After five years, Albert strode into my office again saying, "Don't you think it's time you had a new airplane?"

"No, not necessarily. We're getting along pretty well." I knew that Albert was one who traded cars every two or three years whether he needed to or not.

"Well, isn't it getting kind of old?"

I thought for a moment. "The only thing we need is something with a larger capacity to carry more of the child's stuff."

He made himself at home in the chair in front of my desk. "Well, I don't want you to be without an airplane, so I'll tell you what I'll do. If you find another plane you like, I will loan you the money for it. Then when you sell the Cessna 182, you can pay me back."

Instantly my mind scrambled through the numbers. We'd purchased the 182 for eleven thousand dollars. By the time we replaced the engine and the propeller and upgraded the radios—a memorial gift from my brother's estate after he died in a plane crash—we'd invested about twenty-four thousand dollars. Albert's offer made good sense. Perhaps I should look around at what was currently on the market. I found a used Cessna 206, a six-passenger plane, for twenty-six thousand dollars, which was in much better shape than the 182.

* * *

"I gotta' go!" The young woman in the back seat tapped me on the shoulder. Her face clearly revealed her discomfort. At that moment our little four-passenger plane was flying over the Missouri River Breaks, one of the most desolate areas of Montana. A chaperone and I were bringing Sally back from eastern Montana to her home in Oregon. I looked down and out each window. We were a good forty-five minutes from the nearest airport. I told her our predicament and that she'd have to wait.

She tapped me on the shoulder again, this time more emphatically. "I've got to go—very, very badly!"

I reminded her of the rough terrain we were over. "There's no place to put this baby down."

"But I just have to go—now!"

Remembering a similar trip I'd taken over Winifred, Montana, an old ghost town, I redirected our flight south of the Missouri River Breaks and began searching for the abandoned airstrip with an outhouse near the end. As I approached the airstrip, I could see that it was covered with tall grass. Obviously, the landing strip hadn't been mowed in more than a year. I glanced back at my passenger and then at the grass. By the stress revealed on her face, I knew I didn't have a choice. I would make a descent and land.

As a riot of grass slapped against the plane's windshield and landing gear, I was amazed at how much grass my propeller could mow in the short distance it took us to land. We'd barely come to a stop when the passenger popped the door, leaped from the plane, and dashed across the field to what had once been an outhouse. Two sides of the building had crumbled into a heap of broken two-by-fours, leaving only two sides standing. The chaperone and I turned our heads so she could use the facility in privacy. When she climbed back into the plane, we had to make a couple of runs up and down the runway to mow enough grass so we could take off again.

* * *

On another flight I delivered a young man to the Harris Ranch in Fairfield, Montana, and was flying over to see some folks I knew in Dutton. As we flew, the wind picked up, which wasn't a problem since it was coming from the same direction we were heading. Anyone who has ever flown a plane over Montana knows that the wind there can shift without warning. I was on my last approach on a road that had deep ditches on each side. My main wheels were ready to touch down when the wind shifted, pushing the airplane sideways.

Knowing it would be disastrous to continue my course, I immediately powered to take off. In the process I turned into the wind and managed to jump over the ditch and certain disaster. The plane staggered just above stall speed over a fallow field. By the time we touched down, we were above a wheat field, which slowed the plane quickly. I tried to taxi though the wheat, but couldn't, so I cut the power. When I climbed out, I inspected the plane—no damage except for the stalks of wheat wrapped around the struts of the plane.

The young people flying with me climbed out of the plane and trudged across the field to the nearby home we were visiting. I got back in the plane, started the engine, eased the plane across the next fallow field, and taxied up to the house. Of course I asked the people we were visiting if they owned the wheat field so I could pay them for the damage to their crop.

"No, it's not our field. But we'll tell the owner and ask how much you owe him."

I waited until November and still hadn't heard anything from my friends. Finally I phoned. "Look, I'm still waiting to learn what I owe the wheat farmer for his damaged crop."

The man laughed. "Oh, you don't owe him anything."

"Why not?"

"Well, when he came out and looked at the field, he couldn't figure out how an automobile could completely miss the fallowed field and cut such a clean path through his wheat field. We let him puzzle over it for a time. A couple of weeks ago, he was still talking about the mysterious mode of transportation that had wiped out a section of his wheat.

"Finally I confessed. I told him what happened and that you were willing to pay for the damage. He laughed and said, 'He doesn't need to pay me anything. I'm just so relieved to know what happened. I was almost believing in extraterrestrials and flying saucers. I just couldn't figure it out.' "

* * *

A most remarkable story came from Joan, a woman in Gig Harbor, Washington. She said, "I want you to help me with my daughter."

"What's wrong with your daughter?" Our conversation began like so many others had over the years.

"I can't tell you until you promise you will help me. By the way, I'm not a Seventh-day Adventist, which I understand you are. Will that make a difference?"

"No, it won't make a difference, but tell me, how did you get my number?"

"I don't know. God must have given it to me. But will you help me?"

My curiosity was piqued. "If God gave you my phone number, then I will help you."

"I not only believe you will help me, but I also believe that you are in God's pocket and that He will give you the answers to my dilemma." Her profession of faith in God, in me, and in PATCH touched my heart.

"OK, tell me what's wrong with your daughter."

"Not until you promise me that you will help me regardless of what I say." This woman was persistent. I admired that.

"How can I promise if I don't even know what's wrong?"

"I believe you are in God's pocket."

"But you don't even know me."

"True, but I still believe you are in God's pocket. I'm a woman of prayer and faith. I believe in what you do. Certainly I should be entitled to some crumbs off your floor if you will at least give me a chance and promise to help me."

Her reference to the story of Jesus and the Syrophoenician woman caught my attention. "OK, I'm curious now. I promise to help you."

"Regardless of what I say, you will help?"

"Regardless of what you say . . ."

She took a deep breath before beginning her story. "My fifteen-year-old daughter, Debbie, has been a prostitute since she was eleven. She's deeply involved in a drug and prostitution ring. I've gone down to the brothels of Seattle looking for her time and again only to bring her home, clean her up, and give her a few days' rest and food, and then she's gone again. Today she's in jail, arrested for prostitution. So will you help me?"

"What do you need from me?" I asked.

"I need a safe place for her to live until her trial."

"Isn't jail safe?"

"No. Once the drug and prostitution cartel discover she's been arrested, they'll have one of their other prostitutes get arrested so she can kill Debbie to keep her from turning state's evidence."

"Ooh, I don't know if I can . . ." I didn't like the sound of this at all.

"Wait a minute! You promised that regardless of what I said, you would help me."

Now it was my turn to take a deep breath. "All right. I will help you."

The woman's voice broke with emotion. "Oh, I'm so glad! I believe you're in God's pocket, and I will pray for you. Call me when you find a place for her."

problems, big and small

I hung up the phone and leaned back in my office chair. I didn't know what to do. I couldn't think of anyone who would take a girl who had such a severe issue into their home.

A week later the mother called back. "Have you found a place for Debbie?"

Embarrassed at my inactivity, I stammered a bit before she interrupted. "OK, be honest with me. You haven't even looked, have you?"

"No, I haven't." I hung my head in shame.

"Please don't give up because I know that you're in God's pocket, and I need a place for Debbie immediately."

Reluctantly I agreed to begin looking. Calling around, I found the Averys, a couple in eastern Oregon, who said they'd be happy to take Debbie. They were loggers and agreed to take her into the woods with them for the summer.

I called Debbie's mother with the good news. When I told her about the Averys, she said, "I'm sorry, but that won't work."

"What do you mean 'that won't work'?"

"Trust me, it will not work. But you're in God's pocket, and you'll find the right place because I'm praying for you. I'm a woman of prayer."

"OK, I'll keep looking." I then placed a call to the same people who had taken Sarah a couple years previously. When I told them the situation, they said they'd pray about it and call me the next day."

I was delighted when they called and said they'd take Debbie into their home. Excited, I called Joan and told her about the place I'd found for Debbie. "The terrain is so flat that if she tries to run away, they'll be able to follow her progress for three days!"

"Oh, that's perfect!"

"Do you want to know where it is?"

Joan's reply startled me. "That won't be necessary."

"What do you mean 'that won't be necessary'? Do you mean to tell me that God has already told you where this place is?" By this time I'd come to respect this woman's faith.

"No, that's not it."

"What is it then?" I asked.

"Well, I've been praying that my daughter could go way out of state to protect her, but the state won't allow me to transport her for fear of losing their key witness. They won't allow her to travel by public transportation for fear of endangering other people's lives, and they won't take her anywhere beyond the jurisdiction of the state of Washington." I could almost hear the woman smiling.

"So how do you propose to get her there?"

"I don't know. That's your problem. You're in God's pocket; you figure it out. Call me when you have a solution."

Before she hung up I told her, "Bring her down to Troutdale, Oregon; then I will fly her to Montana, but you have to go along too."

She squealed with delight. "Oh that would be wonderful. I would be happy to go."

By this point, part of me believed this was a real life-and-death situation; the other part of me doubted that it was as serious as the mother claimed. We made an appointment to meet in Troutdale. Everything seemed to be going along without a hitch. Two days later as I headed toward the airport, I was running late. I parked my car and rushed toward the office at the Troutdale airport. I was stopped at the door by a man asking for identification.

"What's so important that I can't come in without identification?" I had flown in and out of this airport on a regular basis. Everyone knew me.

"We have a young lady here who is scheduled to be your cargo. We need to make sure that nobody gets near enough to do her in." The man was a member of Seattle's vice squad. Beyond this massive human barrier, two other detectives sat on each side of a very frightened young girl who I assumed was Debbie.

This was real. Now I was scared. A thousand possible scenarios flashed through my mind. At the moment it seemed like a smart idea to ask the detectives if any one of them wanted to go along.

"Sorry, we have to get back to work. By the way, we need to know where you intend to land en route so we can arrange to have police officers stationed there to make certain there will be no problems during landing, refueling, and taking off again."

"Lewiston, Idaho."

"Sounds good. OK, I think that about takes care of everything. Have a safe flight." The lead detective shook my hand.

"OK." I glanced about the crowded office. "I'll go get the plane."

I taxied my Cessna 182 as close as possible to the building. The mother's eyes widened with fear when she looked at the plane. "Oh dear, is there room enough inside for me? I've never flown in anything smaller than a hundred-twenty-passenger airplane." She inhaled and exhaled sharply. "OK, it's OK. Would it be possible for me to faint once I get strapped in and not waken until we land in Montana?"

"Sure, you do whatever you want just as long as you get in the plane with your daughter," I assured her.

Debbie climbed into one of the rear seats. Her mother sat in the seat beside me. As I prepared for take-off, Joan handed me a fistful of money. "Here, this is to pay for the flight to eastern Montana and back."

I eyed her critically. "Hey, wait a minute. On the phone, didn't you say you had no money? Where did you get this?"

She broke into a broad smile despite her frazzled nerves. "A wonderful thing happened. The vice squad and the district attorney's office were so impressed with my faith that they took up a collection. So now I have the money." The more I learned about Joan, the more impressed I'd become.

Leroy and Linda Bieber were waiting for us when we landed in the pasture adjacent to their home. The next day we went to church with them. During the service, Leroy, a church elder, asked, "Is there anybody here who would like to give a testimony to the Lord this morning?"

Silence followed until Joan stood up. "I would like to thank God for this church." The congregation smiled and nodded at what they interpreted as a casual statement.

Three or four teenage boys about Debbie's age attended the church. Debbie was a most attractive girl, and these young men were eager to greet her and make her feel at home. No one except Joan, the Biebers, and me knew why Debbie was there.

Following church, we attended a potluck twenty or thirty miles outside of town at a church member's cabin on the Fort Peck Reservoir. After lunch Debbie and the four boys went four-wheeling over the countryside. That's when Joan told her story. When she finished, all three mothers of the boys raced to their cars saying, "Where's my son?" The nice part about the church is no one ever brought up Debbie's history to their sons or to her. They treated her with utmost respect.

Three or four months later there was an opening in a wilderness program in western Montana. We arranged for Debbie to spend a few weeks in a wilderness camp. Part of the wilderness experience involved climbing a mountain. Debbie made it part way up the mountain, became frightened, and refused to climb any farther, either up or down. "I'm not moving from here until Tom Sanford rescues me with a helicopter!"

One of the staff members drove to the nearest phone and called Debbie's mother. "Debbie refuses to move until some guy named Tom Sanford comes and picks her up in a helicopter."

Joan called me. "Do you have a helicopter?"

"No, why?"

She explained the situation to me.

I chuckled a bit at the image of this girl clinging to some outcropping of a rock, high over the valley. "You tell the counselor to tell Debbie that she has to go with them, or she has to stay on the side of the mountain because I don't have a helicopter and I can't rescue her."

The counselor delivered my message to her. Stubbornly Debbie refused to move. "I'm still not climbing any farther; someone has to come and rescue me."

They left her with a counselor, all night, on the side of the mountain. The next morning Debbie decided to climb down with the counselor.

Debbie's role as a witness in court against drug dealers turned out well. When the drug dealers learned that she was still alive, safe, and in hiding; when they realized that she would be returning to testify, they fled the country and haven't been heard from since.

*   *   *

Another five years passed during which we logged more than a thousand hours of flight time on the 206. Three events convinced us that it was time to sell that plane too. The first was that Morris Air began selling flights from Portland to Boise for $29—much less money than we could fly the same distance in a private plane. Previously a ticket between the two cities had cost between $250 and $300. Second, because we were required to have fifty million dollars excess liability insurance on the plane, the cost of insurance shot up $10,000 in one year, which seemed like a waste of the donors' money. And third was a string of in-flight mechanical failures, all occurring within one month's time.

The first of the three in-flight problems occurred when Bonnie and I flew from Portland to the ranch in Idaho (more about the ranch later). We knew we'd be landing on the grassy runway in Garden Valley at or near dusk. Though there were no runway lights on the field, we figured that even if it was completely dark, we could see a large tree at the end of the runway and use it as a landing guide to the airstrip. Just as we approached the airport, we both spotted sparks from underneath the dash, followed by a blackout of all the radios and instruments, including the outside lights.

"Hmmph! I don't think I'd better try landing here. It wouldn't be safe. I'd better head for Emmett." I changed our direction and headed for the nearby airport on the outskirts of Emmett.

Bonnie prayed while I flew around the town a couple of times, trying to locate the runway. "Dear God, if we go down, please let the children find our bodies."

Down below, a man leaving the airport in his pickup truck noticed that I was flying without lights. He drove back to the airport and out onto the airstrip, where he aimed his headlights down the runway. His taillights served as a visual reference for the beginning of the runway, thus guiding me to a safe landing. After taxiing in to the terminal, I thanked the man for rescuing us.

"Looks like you might have an alternator problem caused by a short. Is there anything else I can do for you?"

"Yes, could you take us out to the highway? We think our son will be coming in shortly from Portland. He'll pick us up and take us to Garden Valley."

When the gentleman dropped us off at the highway junction, we assured him that someone would be along to get us at any time. Bonnie and I waited beside the loneliest stretch of highway in southern Idaho for less than fifteen minutes before our son arrived. He'd left Portland a few hours before we had.

A short time later, after doing excessive work on the Cessna 206, including replacing an engine, we were hauling concrete equipment and passengers from Garden Valley to Dillon, Montana. With the plane fully loaded and hovering at the gross weight, we taxied down the runway and took off for the steep climb out of the valley. Being at maximum weight, the plane's rate of climb and air speed were limited. But all was going well until blink—the engine quit. It didn't cough. It didn't sputter. It just quit cold.

During the next few seconds I turned the fuel selector valve, hit the boost pump, pressed the starter again, and the engine sprang back to life. Relieved, we flew to Arco, Idaho, where we refilled both tanks. A few weeks later we learned that a clump of dirt had lodged up against the fuel selector valve from the left tank, blocking the fuel supply—a problem created by the craft's former owners.

Once the plane was repaired and again ready to fly, I invited Albert to go with me to Montana to pick it up. Winds whipped across the northern plains, giving us a very bouncy ride home. Albert wasn't feeling too well by the time we reached Hood River.

Going downwind, I throttled all the way back. As I turned left base to land, I lowered the wing flaps to slow my air speed. I then made my final turn to the runway and planned for a little extra power to make certain I maintained a nice gradual descent to the runway. As I eased in the throttle for power, there was none. I tried everything. Nothing worked. I pulled the throttle all the way back and discovered the throttle cable had broken.

I wanted to let my passenger know we were in a serious situation, but he was anxiously looking out the window as if he didn't care how we got down as long as we got down to the ground. I adjusted the wing flaps up to ten degrees and put it in the best angle of descent to give us the greatest possible advantage of making the runway. We skimmed the tops of the pear trees at the end of the runway and nicked a fence before we came to a safe stop on the runway. I knelt and kissed the ground just to make certain we were there.

I had a mechanic look at the plane. "You just put a new engine into this plane, didn't you?"

I assured him I had.

"Any idiot who changes engines knows that you change cables as well. Your cable just broke. I'll charge you a thousand dollars and replace both your cables."

That sounded reasonable to me. A week after we got the plane repaired, I flew home from a meeting in Seattle. Flying high in the clouds, the plane suddenly lost five hundred RPMs.

"Oh, we're in trouble!" I tried to get back the RPMs, but nothing I could do with the prop or throttle adjustment made a difference. "Seattle Central, I'm having some difficulty with my RPMs. I need vectors back down below the clouds."

Praying all the way, I flew under the clouds to Scappoose, Oregon, where I landed safely. Obviously the mechanic at Hood River and the one in Scappoose had attended the same training center. The Scappoose mechanic examined the plane, straightened, and wiped his hands on a rag. "You just had new throttle cables put into this plane, didn't you?"

"Yes, sir, I did."

"Well, any idiot should know that when you change throttle cables, you also change clamps too. Your clamp in the throttle cable broke."

"I appreciate knowing that. I certainly don't want any more idiots in my life, so I think I'll see what else I can do with this airplane."

I contacted Madaline. By this time Albert had passed away. "Madaline, would it be all right with you if I sell the plane and use the money to build duplex housing for the staff at the ranch?"

I was relieved when she responded, "By all means. You are more than welcome to do that if you'd like." After investing forty-two thousand dollars in the plane, I sold it for fifty-two thousand dollars. I thanked the Lord for giving us the use of an aircraft long enough to do what we needed to do and for letting us know when it was time to let it go.

all about
the children

The heart of Project PATCH isn't about planes and finances and generous gifts, as important as they may be. The heart of the program is the children. While Project PATCH officially started on March 1, 1984—the day I severed my employment relationship with the Oregon Conference of Seventh-day Adventists—the ministry began in December 1983. By that time we were fielding a myriad of calls from parents begging us to help them find alternative housing for their children. Walt and Donna Shellman from Hood River housed a number of kids during our first year.

One day Bonnie had gone to the grocery store, and I was restoring an old car in my garage when Walt called, asking to see me.

"Sure, come on down."

A short time later Walt's car pulled into our driveway, and he climbed out of the driver's side. I was surprised to see the young lady who had been staying with them for a couple of weeks sitting in the front seat. Walt rounded the car and opened the passenger door, helped her out, and unloaded her suitcases on the ground beside the car. Uncertain about what was happening, I walked over to greet them.

"Today's my wife's and my anniversary," he began.

"Oh? Congratulations!"

He shook my hand. "I wanted to tell you that I'm giving my wife the best anniversary gift she's ever had."

"That's great." I was really curious where this conversation might be going. "What is it?"

"You're taking this young lady, and she's not coming back with me!"

"What?" I stared dumbfounded.

His eyes and voice were emphatic. "I brought her down to leave with you. That's my gift to my wife today." With that he bid me adieu, got back in his car, and drove away.

Not knowing what else to do, we sat down on the curb, and I asked, "So tell me, what did you do?"

The brown-haired lass, defiance flashing in her eyes, gave the standard teenager's reply. "I didn't do anything."

"Could that be part of the problem?"

"I don't know, and I don't know why I'm here!"

I was to learn that the girl was flabbergasted that anyone would call her on her bad behavior because it had become so normal to her. For the next couple of hours we sat outside, waiting for Bonnie to come home so we could do some planning. We were learning the importance of placing children in a foster home that corresponded a little more with their personal interests and hobbies.

* * *

It was becoming more and more difficult for Jack's mother to manage her son. All he wanted to do was play video games. He didn't want to help out in the home. Everything escalated into an argument. In desperation she brought him to me.

"I need your help. I've run out of options. You need to find a place for him."

I turned to Jack and asked, "What do you see yourself doing when you become an adult?"

He thought for a moment. "What I'd really like to do when I become an adult is to be one of those forest rangers in a lookout tower who spot fires out in the middle of nowhere."

"Do you really think you'd like to do that?"

"Oh, would I ever! I would like that more than anything else in the world!"

I glanced toward his mother and then back at Jack. "Well, we could get you started by living in an environment that would give you the feel of what that life would be like. Would you like that?"

"Absolutely!"

I found Jack a home for the summer in the middle of British Columbia, miles away from the nearest civilization. After one week he called and told me he was bored. He missed his video arcade games. "Up here, you can't even walk a mile for a Camel cigarette because it's ten miles to the nearest store."

"Hang in there, Jack. It's only for the summer. This is giving you the practice you'll need for the memorable day when you'll be a fire spotter for the U.S. Forest Service." Grumbling, Jack hung up and returned to whatever task he'd been assigned.

He called again on the first of July. "I'm bored. There is absolutely nothing here to do. There is no excitement here or near this place."

"You're kidding! There has to be more excitement than what you let on."

At that moment, the foster father picked up the extension phone. "I just wanted to tell you that Jack is having a hard time telling you the entire truth."

I smiled to myself. "How's that?"

"Why, just this morning the dog was barking down by the barn, and I asked Jack to go see why. Jack grabbed his leather jacket—he never goes anywhere without his leather jacket—and moseyed down to the barn. No sooner had he gone behind the barn, but he came charging back to the house. Right on his heels was a big black bear!" The man chuckled. "Jack got halfway to the house, tripped, and fell flat on his face. When he tried to get up, the bear swatted him to the ground, putting a big scratch on the back of his leather jacket. The bear kept running. He was probably more afraid than Jack, I believe. Anyway, Jack can't say he's bored because there's more excitement here than he's probably had his entire life!"

In the wilds of British Columbia, Jack discovered that video games are not real excitement. They're just arcades. Jack still owns the leather jacket with the scratch on it.

Four young men with similar problems came to my attention one summer. They all had similar attitudes and all loved video games. They had no motivation, no goals, no ideals, and no focus in life. For them, life kept happening if they woke up by noon and went to bed whenever they felt like it. They could play games and watch videos round the clock. We at Project PATCH had learned early that improving self-esteem in a child and giving him or her focus is difficult if the child is not motivated to do anything and does not want to venture out in life.

I'd met an adventurous couple who'd talked about spending the summer in Alaska. I asked them if they'd like to take four boys with them. PATCH would pay for their keep. They agreed to meet us at Prince Rupert, where they'd board the ferry to Wrangle, Alaska, and on to Camp Lorraine, where they'd spend the summer on the island.

When we got there, the couple told the boys, "We're going on a great adventure to an island. The only way off is to learn to walk on water; otherwise you're stuck for the entire summer."

As shocked as the boys were, they endured the summer. And without exception each young man has developed a focus in life and become a responsible adult.

* * *

Miracles? Project PATCH is acquainted with miracles. Without exception, every month since we began in 1984, a multitude of miracles have provided the financial basis for the continued operation of the program. As a result, God advanced us from a foster-care placement service to one of the best state-licensed residential child treatment facilities in the Northwest, including school and Joint Council on Accreditation of Healthcare Organizations [JCAHO] accreditation. PATCH progressed from the miraculous $39,000 projected operating costs for the first year to $1.8 million necessary to operate Project PATCH in 2005. It would take reams of computer paper and scores of ink jet cartridges to properly recognize each and every miracle. And every step of the way God proved Himself to be faithful. Here's a few more of the myriad of miracles God sent our way:

By the end of the '80s, fewer and fewer people were willing to take in foster children, thanks in part to a gruesome account of a state foster child killing his foster parents in central Oregon—a case totally unrelated to Project PATCH. As a result, we didn't know which way to turn until a guidance counselor, Paul Campanello, at Columbia Adventist Academy and part-time PATCH employee, suggested that we begin praying for a place of our own.

At the time, the Montana Conference owned property near Seeley Lake, Montana, that had been donated for a youth camp; but the conference had not done anything with it. We proposed to take teens up there to clean up the place and construct some buildings on the condition that the conference would let us use it nine months of the year. In the summer, we would vacate so that they could use the facilities for summer camp. When it went to committee, a few key players thought it was a harebrained idea and persuaded the committee to vote it down. Though frustrated, I knew that God has His hand firmly in everything that we do. I accepted it as His closing one door, knowing He would open another.

I was a bit discouraged because I was still left with the problem of finding homes for children. Willing foster families were few and far between, and they were getting pickier about which children they would take into their homes even though I would try to persuade them otherwise. Reminding myself that God was in control, that He knew the right place for each child, I quit trying to persuade people and turned it over to prayer.

I knew that God knew what we needed and where we needed to be. In June of 1989 both the president and the trust officer of the Idaho

Conference told me that a gentleman in Garden Valley, Idaho, wanted to do something special for young people. Independently, both said, "I think you're the one who should go see him!"

So off I flew into this small mountain airstrip in Garden Valley, Idaho. Sitting in Dan and Margie Rotthoff's living room, which over-looked the South Fork of the Payette River, I had a hard time concentrating on what they were saying: The beauty outside the picture window was enthralling.

Suddenly Dan's words sank into my brain. They wanted to give PATCH their 116-acre ranch on two conditions: First, that they could keep a life estate on the property, and, second, that we would buy the fifty-three acres along the river below their house. Dan went on to explain. "Presently that parcel belongs to Farm Credit Service, but I have the first right of refusal on it. That expires on the first of September, this year. That would give you one hundred sixty-nine acres. That should be plenty of acreage to build a facility for at-risk kids."

He went on to describe the property. "There's a portable log mill, a saw mill, and a pond on that land." He pointed to the river land. "I'll get the saw mill off if you're interested in the property."

Taken back by his generosity and enamored with the beauty of the place, I still had to consider the bottom line. "How much would it cost to buy the fifty-three acres?"

"Oh, about ninety thousand dollars."

I gulped. "Ninety thousand dollars! It doesn't cost us that much to run the entire program every year. We don't have even ten thousand dollars in the bank. I don't know how we'd come up with that kind of money."

Dan was undeterred. "You think about it and pray about it. And if you can come up with it, then maybe we can talk about this a little bit more." This was mid-June. The fifty-three acres had to be purchased by the end of August, or it would be offered for sale to the public.

I returned home, my mind in turmoil. As beautiful as the place was, my faith was weak. *How are we ever going to come up with that kind of money? Besides, I have a couple of board members who might be negative toward this whole idea. Maybe I should poll them before I go any further.*

Immediately I started calling board members. The first board member I called listened to my spiel. "That's not bad. All you need is ninety people to donate one thousand dollars apiece."

I laughed out loud. "Where am I going to find ninety people each willing to give PATCH a thousand dollars?"

"I don't know where you'll get the rest of it, but I'll start the ball rolling by giving you one thousand. Now you have only eighty-nine more donations to raise."

When I explained everything to the second board member I called, she replied, "That's not bad. All you need is nine people to give you ten thousand dollars each."

I was incredulous. "How are we going to find anybody who will give us ten thousand dollars?"

"I don't know, but I'll be the first. I'll give you ten thousand dollars. Now you need to find only eight more people to give you the same amount."

With the commitments of the first two board members in my pocket, I eagerly called the third, hoping he'd say, "That's not bad, all you need is one person to give you seventy-nine thousand dollars." But that didn't happen. However, by polling board members we did raise twenty thousand dollars.

At the mid-July board meeting, someone asked if the property was worth ninety thousand dollars. One of the board members said, "If it proves not to be worth it, I'll buy it, and pay PATCH back. I think it's important to buy this land because the Lord isn't making any more dirt, and property is getting more and more valuable."

The board voted to purchase the land subject to having the money to pay for it. Thirty days before September 1, I received a call from Paul Nelson, the vice president of the North Pacific Union Conference. In a whispered voice, he asked, "Well, do you have the ninety thousand dollars yet?"

"No, but why are you whispering?"

"I don't want anyone in the office to know that I'm calling you."

"OK, I'll be quiet then."

"If you don't have the money now, chances are you won't have it before the first of September. But I've got a way you can get it."

I was all ears. "How's that?" I whispered and then caught myself. Why was I whispering? I wasn't in his office.

"Remember last year when the General Conference made PATCH an official institution of the church? Remember what they said?"

"Yes, they told me the only reason they made PATCH an official institution of the church was because they wanted to add their blessing to the program even though they didn't have the funds to support the program."

"And we couldn't take up offerings in the churches . . ." He finished my thought. "Well, do you know what official institutions of the church are able to do?"

"No, what?" I found myself whispering again, caught in the intrigue of Paul's train of thought.

"They're able to borrow money from the revolving fund for various building projects. You call the union treasurer and ask to borrow seventy thousand dollars. I'll be the one who votes for it, but if you tell anyone I suggested it, I'll deny it. I think it's very important for you to have this property—and this is the way to get it."

As soon as he hung up, I dialed up the union association treasurer, Leroy Reiley. "Hey," I found myself whispering again. Abruptly I switched to my normal voice. "What do I have to do for PATCH to borrow seventy thousand dollars?"

"You'll have to fill out an application and get the chairman of the board or the president of the association to sign it. We'll take a look at it at our next conference committee meeting in the middle of September."

"No, that won't do. We have to have the money by September first."

He cleared his throat. "How do you expect to get it that soon?"

"I don't know, but I'm sure you could find a way we can get the money by that time."

A long pause followed. "OK, you send us the application, and we'll take a look at it."

Along with the signed application, the committee wanted financial statements for the previous couple of months and a complete statement as to what we were going to do with the money. At that time, our financial statement was one sheet of paper—what came in the month previous, what was left over from the month before (usually zero), how much money came in, what we spent the money for and how much was left (another zero). I sent him the requested paperwork and waited a week before calling.

"Well, what do you think?"

In as controlled a tone as possible he replied, "I think Project PATCH has the worst financial statement of any Adventist institution I've ever seen in my entire life! You don't have the ability to pay back seven thousand dollars, let alone seventy thousand dollars!"

Not knowing what else to say, I responded, "So does that mean we get the money?"

He chuckled. "Yes."

"Why?"

I will remember his response for the rest of my life: "We were talking among ourselves, and we are absolutely amazed at what you've been able to do to help children and their families over these last few years. We're also astonished that you've been able to raise so much money through God's strength to keep the program going. We actually thought this whole program would die out within a year. So, we're going to loan you the money because we believe that God is going to give you the money to pay us back."

the miracles continue

The loan came through just in time to purchase from Mr. Rotthoff the fifty-three acres before the first right of refusal expired. When we signed the papers at the end of August, we not only purchased the fifty-three acres but also transferred ownership of the 116 donated acres. It took us until the spring of 1990 to begin developing the property. We hired Monte and Rosie Nystrom, teachers at Mt. Ellis Academy, to be in charge of building roads into the camp and clearing brush. Besides being interested in young people, Monte Nystrom grew up on a ranch in the Bear Paw Mountains outside Havre, Montana. Kids who grow up on ranches don't know the meaning of a nine-to-five day; they work until dark. Also they know how to fix things with bailing wire or a welding rod, if necessary.

The first summer was pretty rough. The Nystroms lived in a twenty-six-foot travel trailer with their three children. The six young people who helped them lived in tents—frigid cold in the mornings and at night; hot the rest of the day. The Nystroms turned an old bathhouse on the property into a makeshift kitchen. Monte used all the scrap gravel that had been stacked around the pond and in an abandoned gravel pit to make roads that were usable year round.

When a woman offered to sell us her doublewide trailer worth thirty-five thousand dollars for fifteen thousand dollars, we bought it on faith. A couple of days later an elderly gentleman wanted to see the place. He had all sorts of questions as to what we were planning to do and how we would do it. While we were talking, I mentioned that we needed fifteen thousand dollars for the trailer and we didn't even have a clue where we'd get the money to move the thing from Medford, Oregon, to Garden Valley.

"Maybe when I leave you'll have a clue." He pulled out his checkbook and wrote a check for fifteen thousand dollars.

I gasped in amazement. What a miracle that he'd showed up at exactly the time that Monte, Rosie, and their children needed a permanent place in which to live.

The Nystroms packed up their three children and the six young people who'd been working with them and headed for Medford, Oregon. Once there, they dismantled the doublewide mobile home by taking off the porches and disconnecting the plumbing and the electricity. Then they hired movers to move the two sections of mobile home to Garden Valley. While they waited for their new home to arrive, Monte built a foundation and dug a trench for the sewer and for the water line by hand. Fortunately someone heard what he was doing and loaned him a backhoe to finish the job.

By October, Monte and Rosie were snugly settled in their doublewide mobile home before winter. And what a winter it was—the coldest one recorded in Garden Valley. Frigid temperatures and twelve feet of snow on the ground!

During that winter and the next, we searched for an architect to draw plans for building a dormitory and a lodge on the property. God led me to Don Kirkman's architectural firm. When I asked him if he would be willing to donate a set of plans for the structure of the youth facility, he said he'd be happy to. The first plans submitted were for a single-level structure with dorm rooms on both sides. After studying the plans, we realized that they weren't totally suitable for our needs. The architectural team graciously redesigned the building. We ended up with a two-story building that looked somewhat homey, with a balcony that overlooked the first floor. We wanted the young people to feel special by providing a relaxing atmosphere that offered privacy without seclusion.

Our next hurdle was the septic system. We didn't know how many septic systems we needed, but we did know that we needed a plan before we acquired the permits for the buildings. Once I had the architectural plans in hand, I contacted the health department for the state of Idaho, which is also the department that issues the permits for septic systems.

I met Marty Jones, the health inspector, out at the property. "The water table is too high here for installing a traditional septic system. You have one septic system here, coming from the bathhouse. It's been here a number of years, and it's not even legal. It looks to me like you'll have to pump the affluent up the bluff and into the pasture." He pointed over his shoulder at the steep incline behind us.

I gazed at the top of the bluff and whistled through my teeth. "Just how expensive will that be?"

"Very. It's probably a quarter to a third of a mile up there."

I groaned. "Isn't there any other possibility?"

Marty's expression told me that while he sympathized with my concern, he could not permit the construction of any buildings by the river without the proper septic system. We had gotten permission to hook up the doublewide mobile home, but beyond that, it looked as if we wouldn't be able to construct any buildings on the fifty-three acres.

"Well, let me think about possible alternatives," Marty offered. He went back to his office to think, and we went back to ours to pray.

Soon after, we received a letter from him. In it Marty stipulated that before he could issue a permit—or even the possibility of a permit—we would need to install a groundwater monitoring system. That involved planting two-inch PVC pipe several feet down in a number of areas. Then once per month over the next year we would monitor the groundwater level and mark it. At the end of the year, they would evaluate it.

A year? We can't do anything for an entire year? I had to do something, anything! I called Marty and asked whether I could meet with him the next time he visited Garden Valley. He agreed. We'd barely sat down to enjoy a breakfast together when he asked, "What do you want?"

Trying to look as casual as possible, I poured maple syrup over my stack of pancakes before I answered his question. "Well, if I understand land-use laws, they change from year to year. What is legal to do this year may not be legal next year."

"Good point. I realize that government bureaucracy takes those turns lots of time. So what do you have in mind?" He eyed me from across the red-and-white checked tablecloth, his fork and knife poised in his hands.

"Since we are doing this groundwater monitoring program as you instructed, could you sign off on it so that we can begin construction before the monitoring program is completed?"

He cut a chunk from his stack of pancakes and chewed it before answering. "Yeah, I suppose so—since it's not a matter of whether or not I'll give you a permit, but what kind of system you're going to use after considering the location of the buildings in proximity to the river."

A grin swept across my face. Suddenly I was starving, and my pancakes were getting cold. Following breakfast Marty signed off on the permit application. Building projects in other states and counties typically demanded six sets of blueprints. After I got my permit and my blueprints together, Bonnie and I hurried to the county courthouse in Idaho City. Feeling ecstatic, I plopped the stack of materials down on the county clerk's desk.

She glanced at the stack of papers and then at me. "And what are these?"

"They're blueprints—six sets!" My chest expanded with pride from a job well done.

"I can see what they are, but why did you bring them here?"

"Don't you need to see the building plans?"

She chortled. "Nobody here reads plans, and I don't want a bunch of plans cluttering up my desk or our office. So get them out of here."

My brow knitted in frustration. "Well, how do we get a permit?"

"Just give us twenty dollars per building, and we'll be happy."

"Is that it?" My amazement registered in my voice.

She glanced at my application. "How many buildings are you constructing?"

"We're building three."

"Hmmm, we already have the permit for your doublewide trailer, so why don't we just add those three buildings to your trailer application and call it good?" She smiled up at me.

In February 1991 I presented the set of plans designed by Don Kirkman's architectural firm to the board. The plans consisted of two dormitories and a lodge. The board examined them and voted to proceed with pouring the foundation. Due to the severity of the winters in Garden Valley, it was impossible to begin excavating and pouring the concrete until April.

Spirits were low on the bitingly cold, rainy day we began pouring concrete. In the process I managed to back into a pier pad and dumped my load of concrete all over myself. The crew doubled over with laughter at the sight. Talk about finding a way to lighten the mood! While we were setting forms, the rural letter carrier delivered a letter containing a check for ten thousand dollars. The enclosed note read, "This check is for the foundation of the new buildings." A month of incessant rain and mud later, we finished the foundations. The bill for the concrete was—you guessed it—ten thousand dollars. Thanks to Arrow Construction from Dillon, Montana, we needed to pay only for the concrete.

As I studied the check, this promise from Philippians 4:19 came to mind: "My God shall supply all your need according to his riches" (KJV). His riches, not mine. God had done it again.

When I reported to the board that the foundations were laid, I asked, "What do you want me to do next?"

One of the livelier members quipped, "What do you usually do with a foundation? You put a building on it! I move that we begin building as soon as funds are available."

As usual, no were funds available. I asked David Anderson, a building contractor, to compile a list of materials we would need. By the end of May, he showed me his list—a small book considering we would need material for three buildings totaling fifteen thousand square feet. With no money in sight, I submitted a list of materials to several lumber companies for a bid. The lowest bid was fifty-five thousand dollars with a five percent discount if paid by the tenth of the month.

"So what does that mean if I order the material by the end of May?" I asked.

"If you wait until the first of June, you have until July tenth to pay for it."

"Would you deliver on June first?" Not one dime was reserved for these buildings. Nor did I know where we'd get the help to frame the proposed buildings.

On June first, the first five semis loaded with lumber rolled down the driveway onto PATCH property. Almost simultaneously the first youth group arrived, directed by Mike and Margie Van Dyke from Medford, Oregon. They arrived the same day the parade of trucks, semi after semi, pulled in with our fifty-five thousand dollars' worth of lumber. By the time the last semi left, the area looked like a giant lumberyard. When the word got out that we were in a massive building program, youth groups with professionals from around the Northwest began showing up to help out. With the help of these volunteers, we were able to enclose both of the dormitories by August. A number of professionals volunteered to come and help finish the walls and add the roof to the lodge.

Bonnie and I spent most of the summer sleeping on site in the back of a donated van. For us this was a trial by fire and ice, due to the cold night temperatures and the high midday temperatures. In the autumn we rented a one-bedroom house for the winter. But, I am getting ahead of my story.

July ninth I asked Marianette, my secretary, how much money we had in the bank. We were short by $700 of having the full $52,250 to pay the bill.

"Great! Write the check!"

"No way." Not a whisper of a smile could be seen on her face. "I've never written a bad check in my life, and I'm not about to write one now."

"Write it!"

"No!"

I couldn't believe her attitude. "Please?"

"I'm not going to jail!"

"Look, I just want to be certain we take advantage of the five percent discount."

"OK, just as long as you promise me two things."

"What's that?" I grinned thinking it couldn't be that bad.

"First, you mustn't deliver the check until five minutes before five tonight. And second, you must promise me that seven hundred dollars will come in the mail by tomorrow morning."

"I can do that! God hasn't failed us yet. Why would He start now?"

The next morning both of us rejoiced when we opened the mail and found checks totaling seven hundred dollars.

Midsummer the fire marshal arrived to inspect our framed-up buildings. "You need a sprinkler system for fire protection in all the buildings."

"I can't imagine that would be a problem. We can just dig a line to the river and pump the water out of the river."

He shook his head even as I spoke. "Not so, because of all the sand and sediment. There is no guarantee you'd get adequate water in the winter when the river is low and perhaps frozen."

"How about taking the water from the pond?"

"Same problem."

I tried every suggestion I could with the fire marshal to minimize our cost. And while he was kind, he was emphatic. "You need a reserve tank that feeds from the well."

Defeated I asked, "How big of a reserve tank do we need?"

"I'd say a minimum of a twelve-thousand-gallon tank."

Since a gallon of water weighs eight pounds, just the water alone would weigh ninety-six thousand pounds. What size tank will it take to hold that much water? We ordered a twelve-thousand-gallon tank that weighed twelve-thousand pounds itself—a pretty hefty project—and then we needed the concrete for support. Dennis Simpson of Arrow Construction figured we'd need ten yards of concrete just as a base for the two ends of the twelve-thousand-gallon tank. Without the cost of the tank or building to house the tank, the sprinkler system would cost us seventy-five thousand dollars—and we couldn't proceed with the building project until we installed a sprinkler system.

I did the only thing I could do: order the system on the philosophy of the board, "If you pour the concrete for the foundation, the next step is to build a building." And then we prayed, asking God to once again provide the money. Again He proved, "Surely the arm of the LORD is not too short to save, nor his ear too dull to hear" (Isaiah 59:1, NIV). The day we received the bill for the sprinkler-system installation, we received a check for seventy-five thousand dollars to cover it.

With the sprinkler system installed, we were ready for the next step, the plumbing. Douglas Roe, one of our employees at the time, went to town to see what kind of deal he could make with some plumbers. When he shared Project PATCH's story with Milford Terrell, the owner of DeBest Plumbing, he asked whether Milford would be able and willing to give us a discount on the plumbing. Mr. Terrell did one better. He polled his employees and asked them whether they would be willing to spend a day or two installing the plumbing in three buildings in Garden Valley. The project included seven kitchens and twenty bathrooms, sixteen of which had showers, tubs, or shower/tub units. On the designated day, Milford Terrell's employees arrived en masse, and in one day all of the plumbing was finished. So many plumbers moved so fast you couldn't count them.

Following the state licensing in December, the young people moved into the dorms. As I watched the process, tears glistened in my eyes. *What a sight! What a blessing! Look what God has done!*

Along with the blessings and miracles that arrived, came a problem or two as well. One building on the campus did not come as a result of volunteer labor—the 40 × 80–foot shop. We contracted with a pole building company to build it for us. A month after we paid our final installment on the shop, we received a surprise in the mail—a mechanic's lien on our property. The contractor who built our shop had failed to pay for the concrete he'd purchased from Lowe's Redi-mix—and he had left town.

Facing a four-thousand-dollar bill for the second time, I was filled with apprehension when I went to Lowe's Redi-mix to explain our predicament. The owner courteously listened and then said, "If you'll pay just two thousand dollars, we'll forgive the rest."

A week later I delivered the two-thousand-dollar check to them. As I was about to leave, the owner called me back to say, "We support a lot of nonprofit organizations. If you ever need concrete again, let me know."

Six years later I did as he suggested. I went back to order one hundred yards of concrete for the floor of our school. As I sat in the owner's office, choking on his cigarette smoke, I was so uncomfortable I considered leaving without talking with him. It had been a long time since I'd inhaled that much secondary smoke. Instead of leaving, I decided to endure the discomfort. We needed concrete, and the normal delivery rate for a remote place like Garden Valley was eighty-five dollars a yard plus travel and waiting time.

I extended my hand in greeting, barely choking back a cough. "I'm here to take you up on your offer."

He remembered me. "Great! What do you need?"

"About a hundred yards of concrete."

"OK, I'll do what I promised."

I wasn't sure what that meant, but I was eager to listen.

"How about I charge you for materials, but not for delivery or the mix?"

I grinned and nodded. "Sounds good to me!"

When we received the bill it amounted to less than three thousand dollars—a blessing indeed!

When we began Project PATCH in 1984, our annual operating budget was $39,000. The first year, Bonnie volunteered her time working as my secretary. The board voted to begin paying her for her time, but since the finances weren't coming in, she received five dollars per hour. We also hired Paul Campanello as a counselor, subject to the funds available. But the funds weren't coming in. Since we'd made a commitment to Paul, we hired him anyway. And then the funds began arriving. When Paul quit and returned to teaching full time, we hired two other employees, Linda Logan and Lynette Anderson—one part time and the other full time—and again the funds arrived to cover their salaries. By 1989 our annual operating budget had increased to a hair over $100,000, an amount that to us seemed phenomenal. With the building of the ranch and hiring staff to run it, the budget kept growing. And before we knew it, it was costing us $1.8 million annually.

A friend of mine pointed out that I could put up a child at Holiday Inn and feed him or her three nice meals a day, and it would cost less than it cost per child at Project PATCH. I reminded him that the accounting might be true, but the end result would be a child only housed and fed. From the beginning, PATCH's focus has been to improve young people's self-esteem and to help improve the quality of their lives. How can one put a price tag on helping teenagers learn to make positive choices that will enable them to find jobs and to develop healthy personal relationships and a spiritual purpose in their lives?

When we needed skilled labor to make the large trusses in the lodge, people arrived who knew exactly how to do that. Unfortunately, we couldn't get the roof finished before the winter snows fell. As a result, some of the lumber ended up a little wet, but nothing needed to be replaced.

At the end of the summer when we'd run out of youth groups, Maranatha volunteers showed up. Maranatha Volunteers International is a nonprofit Christian organization that uses volunteers to construct buildings, such as schools, churches, and hospitals, throughout the world. More than fifty thousand people have volunteered for Maranatha projects since 1969. A group had just finished a project in

Coquille, Oregon. Some of the crew from that project came to Project PATCH to help frame the building. Joyce and Ken Casper, on the governing board of Maranatha, later made a trip to see the ranch. They arranged to have the organization come the following summer to help us construct a duplex for staff housing, as well as finish the core building to use as a kitchen.

A group of volunteers from Maranatha has been at Project PATCH every summer from 1991 to 2001. They skipped 2002 and 2003 but returned in 2004 for more sprucing up. Had it not been for those volunteers, we might still be in the bare-wall stages of the projects. After the first duplex, they finished the lodge and built a second duplex, an office, a barn, a storage shed, a school, and ultimately, a chapel in 2005. Maranatha volunteers have been heaven sent.

the miracle ranch

In December 1994, one year after we opened our doors, Project PATCH was again in serious debt. PATCH had only recently been licensed and approved by the state.

We'd been in debt before, but never to the amount we were facing this time. And there was no sign of things getting better. By the December board meeting, we knew the ministry was at an important crossroads. I could feel the knots building in my stomach as I reported our situation to the board members.

I began my report with the bad news that by the end of the year, if the trend continued, we would be in debt over $150,000. "We won't even have the money to pay salaries. And we'll be forced to lay off employees," I continued. I felt nauseated, for I knew that all of the people working for PATCH had such a heart for the young people in their charge. "One alternative would be to close one of the dormitories. This would save us some money and maybe recoup some of our losses.

"If we close the girls' dorm, we will be forced to send home a couple of girls who have been sexually abused. These girls aren't talking about what has happened to them. According to law, you can't have an offender if you don't have a victim. As things are, we can't help them in any way other than by providing a place to stay." I swallowed hard. "If we close the boys' dorm, we're sending home one young man in particular whose stepmother wishes he were dead or would rather see him living on the streets than to have him come back home. Another young man currently with us is in an equally difficult situation due to physical abuse." I dropped my head for a moment before continuing. "I don't know what to say. Please tell me what I should do."

A long pause followed until Rick Negus, the assistant regional manager for children's services in eastern Oregon who had been on the board since PATCH's inception, leaned forward in his chair. He was also a personal friend who'd helped us pilot JAM from the start. "When I first joined the board, I was not a Christian. Prior to joining the board I didn't have a lot of faith, but in the past ten years I've observed all the miracles that have kept PATCH going. God has continually provided through very tenuous situations and difficult financial times. Look at the miracles that have occurred just putting together the ranch."

His gaze swept around the table. "I am a fiscal conservative. By profession, I have to be a fiscal conservative. To be frank with you, if we were all in my position, I would be surprised if we didn't all end up in jail!" He uttered a sardonic chuckle. "As far as the state is concerned, you just don't spend money you don't have. So what I am about to say contradicts my personal philosophy and my professional opinion." He took a deep breath.

"I believe that if God has given us the finances in the past and established a track record of blessing and the faith for PATCH to continue on, then I would like to recommend that we do not stop at this time. We need to keep on keeping on and trust that God will give us the money for the bills so that we can continue into next year and beyond."

Later I learned that Rick had become a Christian based on the evidence of what he'd seen while working with Project PATCH. When he ended his testimony, each of the board members told of their personal experience with Project PATCH. Several admitted that, as professional business people, they would never even consider running their business the way Project PATCH runs. Yet they all agreed that perhaps God has a different set of rules by which He wanted them to play. They voted to "keep on keeping on" and to pray that the money would come when it was supposed to and not one second sooner.

After the board had voted, we prayed that God would provide the money to allow us to continue the program and continue to keep both dormitories open. If He would choose not to honor our request by virtue of the merits of the request alone, that He would honor our requests to strengthen the faith of Rick Negus.

I left the meeting on a cloud of enthusiasm. I decided that I should do my part in letting people know of our need. First, we tried to get permission to do some mass mailings, but were turned down. Christmas was coming, and we were still far short of the necessary funds to begin a new year.

Scheduled to speak at a small church in southern California on Saturday afternoon, I knew that a lot of church members wouldn't show up for the meeting. So I called the pastor of the Calimesa Seventh-day Adventist church and told him I was to be in the area. "I would be happy to make a presentation to your congregation as well."

"I am sorry, but we don't invite outside speakers. Our board of elders is made up of university professors and retired General Conference officers. We have more than enough speakers within our congregation."

"How about at Sabbath School?"

"No, I'm afraid not. On that Sabbath we're having somebody from Russia speak—so that won't work either."

I was getting desperate. "How about during the announcement period?"

"Sorry, but we don't use our announcement time for promotional purposes. I am sorry, but we can't use you at this time."

Feeling frustrated, I made one last effort. "Would you mind letting me know if you change your mind or have a schedule change? I'll be staying with Dave and Janet Wilkins. So if there's a change in the schedule, I would be happy to speak at your church."

When I arrived at the Wilkinses' home on Thursday evening, I'd barely walked in the front door when the phone rang. It was the Calimesa church pastor.

He got right to the point. "I have the flu, and I seriously doubt that I will be able to make it to church this week. I was wondering if you would be able to take both services for me?"

I readily agreed. I hung up before I carried out the temptation to ask him what had happened to his associate pastors and his board of elders. But God had given me the opportunity, and I thought I'd better not question it further.

On Sabbath morning I spoke to a full house. Between services one of the deacons confided, "You hit the church at the ideal time." I asked what he meant. He explained, "This is the largest number of people I've seen in all the time I've been a member, and that's a number of years."

Not only did Project PATCH receive a positive financial response from the congregation that day but we also received a $7,000 grant from a large foundation. Between December 10 and 31, God directed $160,000 into PATCH's coffers—the exact amount of our outstanding bills. On the first Sabbath of the New Year, I stood and sang with re- newed enthusiasm, "Great is Thy faithfulness, O God my Father . . ."

Eternal lessons must be learned again and again—at least in my case. I can't help but wonder why I can't learn them the first time through like so many others claim to do.

By the third week of August 1995, I was ready for another dose of God's miraculous provision. Sitting on a sofa in my office at the ranch, I stared at the mountain of bills and payroll expenses, totaling more than forty thousand dollars, on my desk across the room. Besides the lack of funds, it had been a summer filled with staffing problems and criticism coming at me from every corner.

Dropping the magazine I'd been reading, I buried my face in my arms and prayed the same prayer I'd been praying throughout the dif- ficult summer. "Oh God, these are Your kids, not mine! If You're not interested in what happens to Your children, why should I be?"

The idea of running far, far away and starting over where no one knew me so that I wouldn't need to worry about God's kids anymore appealed to me more and more the longer I held my head in my hands. Yet every time I played with the idea, I remembered Jonah. "Please don't treat me like Jonah," I pleaded. "I haven't done anything wrong. If you're not going to send the money necessary for operating this program, please respect my wishes and let me go!"

Before I could whisper an "Amen," one of the girls burst through the closed door. "Jamie!" I started. We tried to train the children to knock before they entered someone's private room or office. The girl barged right in and plopped herself down across from me. I didn't want to talk with her or anyone else at that moment because I was formulating my plan to run away. Trying to clear the tears from my eyes that were threatening to streak down my face, I picked up my magazine and resumed reading, or at least pretended to read it.

"Can I sit beside you?" she asked.

Inwardly I groaned. But out loud I said, "I guess so. Why not?"

Jamie jumped up, and instead of sitting on the far end of the sofa, she sat down so close that she hurt my hip as she sailed down beside me into the softness of the cushion.

I kept on reading, or at least, pretending to read, trying to ignore her presence. After a short silence she asked, "Are you rich?"

"What makes you think I'm rich?" I ached to tell her to leave so that I could continue pouting, but I couldn't bring myself to do it.

"All of the kids around here say you built this ranch for kids like me. Nobody would consider doing something like that unless they were rich and didn't have anywhere else to spend their money!"

I smiled at the irony of her accusation and thanked her for the compliment. "As a matter of fact, I'm not rich. Financially I am very poor. This place exists because a lot of people have given their money and their time to build it just for kids like you."

"But aren't you rich anyway?"

I stared at her brashness and apparent insight into the tortures of my own soul. "Yes, I am very rich because you are here."

Tears spilled from her eyes. She jumped to her feet. "You're right! You're rich because of the fact that since I've been here, I've had no desire to do drugs. I haven't wanted to kill myself. And I don't want to sell my body anymore!" With that she turned and ran out of the door.

The door slammed behind her as if adding the exclamation point to God's timely lesson.

Philippians 4:19—"My God shall supply all your need according to his riches"—flashed through my mind. "Forgive me, Father, for doubting!" I leaped up from the couch and ran to my desk to send out forty thousand dollars' worth of checks, knowing there was absolutely nothing to cover them except the faith that God would provide.

On the Tuesday following Labor Day weekend, I was back in Portland and anticipating the miracle God had promised. It didn't come. In fact, only a little over three hundred dollars came in the mail that day. If my situation was bad before, now it was worse. I was no longer stranded out on a limb; I had just sawed it off!

Carefully I ran my conversation with Jamie through my mind again. What had I missed? Was God trying to give me a different message as far as the ranch was concerned? I fell to my knees. "Tell me, Lord, what You would have me do!"

When I rose to my feet I had the distinct impression that I needed to get out and solicit money again. "Whom, Lord, would You have me contact?"

The very first person I went to see came running out of his house as I pulled into the driveway. He greeted me with, "Boy am I glad to see you!"

I blinked in surprise. "Why?"

"I couldn't sleep all night."

"Really?"

"Yeah. I have fifty thousand dollars in the bank, and God is convicting me to do something with it. It kept me awake all night! Finally at five this morning the answer came to me."

By this time my smile filled my face from ear to ear. I knew what God had told him to do. Why had I ever doubted? "What did God tell you to do with the money?"

"Well, I knew that my neighbor is about to lose his house, so I'm going to loan the money to him so he can refinance his place and have a chance to keep it."

My mouth dropped open in surprise. I couldn't think of a thing to

say. I'd been so certain that God had intended to solve my own dilemma with this man's money.

Suddenly the man stopped and looked questioningly at me. "By the
way, what did you stop by for?"

I inhaled sharply. "Oh, nothing. I don't really have anything important to talk with you about—I was just in the area and came to say hi."
I was stuttering and stumbling all over myself. My rescue came when
someone else drove into the man's driveway.

Befuddled with the strange turn of events, I said Goodbye and
drove to the home of the next people on my list, and the next. No one
was home. Discouraged, I drove home thinking, *Why don't I just kill
myself and get it over with?* I confided my thoughts to Bonnie.

"I might as well go to McDonald's and get the biggest and greasiest
order of French fries and eat them all. That should do it! I'll kill myself
with high cholesterol!" *What am I thinking? That would be a slow death.
The checks will bounce long before the cholesterol level proves fatal!*

That afternoon when I returned to my Portland office, Marianette,
my secretary, greeted me with the news that I needed to call a certain
gentleman. "He's been calling all day."

"I don't want to talk with anyone today," I mumbled, feeling totally
sorry for myself. "Besides, no one calls me to do something nice for me." I
strode into my office and closed the door. Behind me the door swung open.
Marianette stood in the doorway with her arms folded across her chest.

"If you don't call him today, you'll have to call him tomorrow," she
reminded.

"Hmmph! Guess I'd better give him a call then. I don't want to
waste my one phone call from jail on him."

I settled into my desk chair and dialed up the number. "Hello, this is
Tom Sanford returning your call." I sounded much cheerier than I felt.

"So how is PATCH going?"

I immediately shifted out of my bad attitude into my public rela-
tions pose. "Fine, just fine. The kids are doing very well. You wouldn't
believe the miracles and transformations in their lives." I lied. Nothing
was going well.

He saw through my evasion and zeroed in on the problem. "So how are the finances?"

"Not so well." I couldn't admit to him how far we were in the red and how weak my faith was at the moment. "Tell me, would you consider loaning us twenty thousand dollars?" I thought I'd soften the blow by asking for a loan as opposed to a gift, and a loan for only half of what we needed.

"Absolutely not!"

I was taken back by his adamant response.

"Why?"

"Because I'd never get it back, that's why! I wouldn't loan you two hundred dollars for the same reason. I wouldn't loan you twenty dollars. In fact, I wouldn't even loan you two dollars!"

"OK." I conceded, figuring that was the end of the conversation.

"But I will give you forty."

"Forty dollars?"

"No, I'll give you forty thousand dollars. My question is, Do you need it or don't you?"

I felt as if someone had knocked the wind out of me. "You bet I need it! You can't imagine how desperately I need it!"

I then told him about mailing out forty thousand dollars' worth of checks. "We need the money in the bank by tomorrow to keep them from bouncing."

"Fine, I'll put it in the mail today."

"No, no! I'll come by and pick it up if it's all right with you."

"Sure." I grabbed my car keys and dashed out of the office. It took me until midnight to drive to his home and back. When I asked him why he decided to give us forty thousand dollars, he said, "At nine o'clock this morning I got my mail. In one envelope was a substantial check that was owed to me, one I never anticipated seeing. As soon as I saw it, I dropped to my knees and asked God what He would have me do with the money. PATCH popped into my mind." He was grinning from ear to ear. "That's why I asked you if you needed it. If you hadn't, I would have questioned whether or not my first impression was God's will."

Nine o'clock—that's when I left on my frantic search for money. Shame on me! I had doubted, but God had come through again.

*   *   *

When I think of Marci and her grandmother, I remember the promise in God's Word that says, "Cast thy bread upon the waters: for thou shalt find it after many days" (Ecclesiastes 11:1, KJV). During her teenage years, Marci needed PATCH's help. Neither her father nor her mother had the money or interest to support her. We found a sponsor for her at Project PATCH, and Marci stayed with us at the ranch for almost a year.

Several years later, Marci's grandmother called me from her hospital bed and asked me to come see her. When I did, she said, "You know I'm here in the hospital because I'm sick and about to die. I would like to give PATCH twenty-five percent of my assets when I pass away, but I don't have a will. Could you have someone write up one for me?"

"Sure, but are you sure you're going to die?"

"I am certain I am about to die. There is no doubt about that."

The next day a person from the Oregon Conference trust department and I went to get the necessary information to draw up the papers. That afternoon Marci's grandmother phoned again; she was anxious to get the job done quickly. I called the trust people and told them the paperwork had to be done by the following day. Because her son would be the one who would be the recipient of her estate, they felt it was important to determine that he had no objections to his mother giving away 25 percent of the estate. The son agreed and signed the necessary papers on Friday. The woman passed away on Saturday night.

Later at the funeral her son, Marci's father, confided, "I didn't pay you one red cent for caring for my daughter. I'm just happy that Mother gave you the twenty-five percent she did. I would have agreed to fifty percent, but since she's gone, I'm not going to give you the other twenty-five percent."

Sometimes Project PATCH's financial needs were met in a most roundabout way.

money, miracles, and more

Chapter 13

With most of the construction completed on the buildings, we turned our attention to the pond. Monte had used all the piles of gravel around it to build the roads. But we still had one problem with the pond: The old gravel pit opened into the river. As a result, the water in the pond rose and fell with the elevation of the river. Some days it looked like a beautiful pond; other days it resembled a muddy swamp. In the summertime, beavers successfully dammed the entrance to the river, but when river level rose after a rain, their dams washed out.

I contacted the same engineer who designed our septic system and asked him about the possibility of building a dam. "Well, since the river is a protected waterway, you're going to have to get a permit from the U.S. Army Corps of Engineers," he pointed out.

I contracted with him to design a dam, and then I submitted it to the Corps of Engineers. They, in turn, published the permit application for other agencies. All of the agencies that responded approved after we answered one or two questions—all except for the Department of Environmental Quality (DEQ) and the Department of Fish and Wildlife. The Corp of Engineers told me that they wouldn't issue the permit until I satisfied the objections of both the DEQ and the Department of Fish and Wildlife.

The DEQ's concern was that the location of the dam and the pond was too close to an existing waterway. The Department of Fish and Wildlife's concerns were with the aquatic flow from the pond should we build our dam. The area was also bald eagle winter range, and we could do nothing that might endanger the habitat. As a result, it was decided that if we wanted to build a dam, we would need to move the entire project at least 100 to 150 feet from the river.

After reading their report, I called the Department of Environmental Quality and asked them to further explain their objections to the location of the pond and the dam.

"We wrote out our objections. And we are pretty emphatic about the fact that you are way too close to the river."

I had to admit that in some spots the only separation between the river and the pond was a narrow dike, barely ten feet wide. "Have you ever been out to examine the pond?"

The voice on the other end of the telephone sounded impatient. "No, I don't have to. Our job is to respond to the application."

I took a deep breath. "OK, tell me something. Have you ever tried to move a gravel pit?"

"What do you mean, 'move a gravel pit'?"

"What we want to do is dam up the end of a gravel pit that opens into the river."

A long pause followed. "Oh, I see. You mean the pit is already there, and you just want to dam it up?"

"Exactly."

Another long pause followed. "Well then, I guess we don't have any objection. I apologize for suggesting that you move the gravel pit."

The woman at the Department of Fish and Wildlife again stated her objections. When she finished I asked her, "Have you ever been to the project?"

"No." Her voice sounded a trifle snappish. "It's my job to object to these types of things. I don't have to be there to know that it's not the appropriate thing to do."

I pressed my point. "So then you aren't aware that the beavers are trying to dam the spot themselves and are struggling with it? Every time the river rises, the water backflows into the pond or gravel pit, and they are washed out."

"Well, that's too bad. Let them continue to struggle!"

I injected as much kindness as I could into my voice. "I'll make a deal with you. If you refuse to let us build a dam, I will import more beavers to give them a greater chance to build their dam. It won't look as nice as the one we'd build, but at least we'd have a dam."

"Tsk! You would actually import beavers to do this?"

I chuckled at the surprise in her voice. "Exactly. We want a dam at the end of that unsightly gravel pit—and you're objecting to it."

I heard a deep sigh on the other end of the phone. "Well, if you promise not to import any more beavers, I'll approve your project."

We got our permit. When the dam was built, the beavers moved to another site and quit cutting down our young cottonwoods. I was so thankful that, throughout the entire construction process, God gave us the wisdom and the ability to communicate with all the agencies involved with the project: the fire marshal, the health department, the Department of Health and Welfare, the state electrical inspector, the plumbing inspector, the Department of Idaho Water Resources Board, Idaho Parks and Recreation, the DEQ, the Friends of the Payette, the Department of Fish and Wildlife, and the Army Corp of Engineers.

We never hid anything from the agencies or tried to manipulate facts. Throughout the process, the departments mentioned time and again that they were appreciative of our cooperation while working with them.

* * *

The events of 9/11 hit Americans hard. The resulting ripples fanned out far beyond the immediate victims and their families. With the economy in decline, discretionary giving was already at a low. And then with the tragedy, financial gifts were redirected to families of the 9/11 victims. PATCH's income decreased by more than thirty-five thousands dollars a month.

Determined not to close our doors, we prayed for guidance. Mark

Driscoll, our development director at the time, contacted one of our donors who gave once a year. Mark asked him about the possibility of providing additional support to get us to January and February of 2002. The donor promised to think about it and get back to us.

A few days later Mark received his call. "I've thought and prayed about it. And I've concluded that the best thing I can do for Project PATCH is to give two dollars for every new dollar you raise. That's new dollars, not regular money from your regular donors."

Our spirits soared! We began contacting people and were surprised at the creative responses we got. By the end of February of 2002, we had $89,000 of "new money" to meet our two-for-one challenge. The donor ended up contributing $178,000 to the program. That, along with our regular donations, carried us through the month of June.

Time and again God showed us that PATCH was His project, not ours. He reminded us that He is in control.

In the spring of 2003 we were again thirty-nine thousand dollars in the hole. Again I sent out payroll checks on Friday and prayed that the money would come in to cover them before Monday. This time it didn't. By Tuesday, my spirits plummeted when I was notified that we had insufficient funds to cover a couple of checks that had already arrived at the bank.

Tired of the battle, I didn't feel much like talking to God about it. We had had this conversation so many times in the past. With nothing else to do, I decided we should continue on with our normal office routine of worship and prayer. When I arrived, one of the staff members was reading a devotional. I slunk into the room and found an empty chair. By the scowl on my face, anyone would know I wasn't my usual upbeat self that morning. In fact, I was mad at God for not providing the money when I believed we needed it most. And I was in no mood to be civil with Him.

I glanced around the room to determine whose turn it was to offer the morning prayer. The more I listened to the devotional reading, the more I knew that if I was the one with the issue with God, then I was the one who needed to talk about it. At the end of the reading, I asked if anyone had any special requests. After listening to each request, I admitted to my staff, "I have a request to make this morning. We are in a particularly difficult financial situation." Only the accountant and I knew how bad it was. "We desperately need some money to come in today. Let's bring the problem before the Lord today."

As we bowed our heads to pray, I prayed, "God, You know what a financial mess we're in right now—and that's all I'm going to say about the situation." I paused at the jangling of the telephone in the corner of the room and waited while Jerry, our accountant, answered it.

Quietly he whispered "Yes," and "Thank you." When he hung up the receiver, he had tears in his eyes. "Before they call, I will answer . . ." Our petition time turned into one of gratitude and praise. Jerry reported that the caller had just phoned to say that he was overnighting twenty-five thousand dollars to us. He had no knowledge of the difficult situation Project PATCH was in.

First Peter 5:6, 7 sprang into my mind. "Humble yourselves, therefore, under God's mighty hand, that he may lift you up in due time. Cast all your anxiety on him because he cares for you" (NIV). Conscience-stricken, I bowed my head and acknowledged His Lordship over me and over Project PATCH.

Time and time again I've had to relearn that God seldom chooses to give more than we absolutely need at any given point. And though I've been upset with Him because of difficult circumstances and because He seems to respond so slowly to our needs, I have to acknowledge that it is His job to provide, not mine. Even though we find it so difficult to pray and wait—"Be still and know that I am God"—He does love us and knows what is best for us. And though I am a glacially slow learner when it comes to trusting, I can see that He is busy perfecting my character through each of these trials.

By now, I am certain no one can imagine the growth of PATCH has been a joy-filled canter from one field of daisies to the next. Financial issues were but one of the series of crises facing us. Another has been staffing issues. Hiring the right person for each position proved to be more of a challenge than I'd ever imagined. I always believed myself to be a perceptive individual, and I thought I could accurately size up qualified applicants. I learned that being a parent of a half dozen grown children is not a reliable guarantee that he or she is a good prospect to work as part of a team.

I often found myself blinded by a great personality and a stated love for kids. The result was that I spent an inordinate amount of time dousing brush fires among the staff. Several mistakes later, members of my faithful staff came to me much like Jethro came to his son-in-law, Moses. "You need help. You can't expect to do it all and know it all." Together we developed an interviewing process that helped weed out unqualified candidates. Besides the obvious interview where we discovered whether or not the candidate had recently been involved with drugs or alcohol or charged with assault against either an adult or a minor, we came up with a four-day experience of interacting with our staff and clients to discover how much of a team player the individual might be.

Knowing that Christ has believers in other denominations as well as our own, we took the position that we would hire employees from any denomination who demonstrated a healthy relationship with Christ. Our only spiritual stipulation was that Jesus Christ must be the person's primary focus in any discussion with a child. An expression of anger was never to be spoken or displayed in front of a child. Enough anger had been directed at these kids in their short lives. Our goal was to show them a better way through positive interactions.

Today PATCH has more than forty employees at the ranch, ministering to an average of thirty-two young people. At work they all uplift Jesus Christ—regardless of the diversity of denominational beliefs. Each staff member believes that his or her presence is a miracle. And every miracle story bears retelling.

Take the one that began in Spray, Oregon. Six months in advance I'd been invited to speak at the local Seventh-day Adventist church. The last thing the individual asked before hanging up the phone was, "Now, you promise you will come, won't you? Most of the time people accept our invitation and then, at the last minute, cancel on us."

I assured the woman I would be there. I always maintain that the size of the church has no bearing on my schedule. I was there to speak to

God's people, regardless of the number. However, the week prior to the appointment I was overwhelmed with work. I was looking forward to a quiet weekend at home when I remembered my promise to go to Spray.

"Bonnie, I really don't want to go. I'm just too tired."

Her response was immediate. "We are going regardless of how tired you are. You promised, and they're expecting you."

So much for sympathy! After learning there were no motels in Spray, we decided to drive to Condon, stay overnight and continue on early Sabbath morning. On Friday evening we arrived in Condon to discover that the only motel in the town was completely booked by hunters.

Relieved, I sauntered back to our car, carefully concealing my eagerness to cancel our trip from Bonnie. We couldn't go on, not without a place to stay for the night. We'd have to return home.

"Isn't there any other place in town where we can stay?"

"You don't understand, Bonnie; this is the only motel. The desk clerk assured me that this is the only motel and all rooms are booked." Bonnie could be insistent at times.

Without warning, Bonnie hopped out of the car and dashed inside the motel office. It must have been the determined look on my wife's face because the desk clerk suddenly remembered, "There's a guy in town who bought a singlewide trailer, and he's willing to rent it out."

We waited while the motel clerk phoned half the citizens of the town, or so it seemed to me. Finally she located the owner of the trailer and arranged for us to rent it for the night. Even though she gave us the wrong directions to the trailer, the town of Condon is so small it was still relatively easy to find.

The next morning we arrived at the church in Spray to discover that half the congregation was away for the weekend. After the service the four members in attendance and the four visitors, including Bonnie and me, went to a church member's home for lunch. Over the customary potluck fare, one of the other visitors told a story about a Seventh-day Adventist aunt of his who lived in Marysville, Washington.

"She loves the Baptist minister's sermons so much that she goes to the Adventist church on Sabbath and attends a Baptist church on Sundays." Stirring the taco-salad ingredients on my plate, I was only half-listening until the man said, "My aunt's frustrated because the local Baptist board of elders fired their minister because of his wife."

I glanced over at the visitor. "What's wrong with the minister's wife?"

"Oh, she became a Seventh-day Adventist. The board of elders told him that he either had to set his wife straight or lose his job."

"Really?" I arched my eyebrows in surprise. "Apparently he couldn't straighten her out."

The man shook his head. "He didn't even try. He told his board of elders, 'How can I ask my wife to give up something that has brought her true happiness?' So they fired him. He'd grown their church from a small congregation to more than six hundred members too!"

The possibility of a new staff member entered my mind. Now I understood why Bonnie had been so insistent we keep our speaking appointment. "Can you get me the minister's phone number?"

"Sure." The man seemed surprised. "But it may take me a few days."

Despite being given a wrong number, I contacted Pastor Jim Smith a couple of days later. I introduced myself and asked him if the story I'd heard on Saturday in the remote town of Spray, Oregon, was accurate. He assured me that it was and that he had no regrets for standing up for his wife's beliefs.

I could feel my enthusiasm mounting. "How would you like to come and work for us?"

"What do you do?"

Jim listened politely as I explained about Project PATCH. A long pause followed before he responded. "If you were to ask me to list everything I could see myself doing in life, dealing with troubled children would not be anywhere on that list. But thanks for asking. I'm going to apply to work for World Vision or Multnomah School of the Bible."

"Why don't you come and see what we're all about before you say no," I coaxed. "It couldn't hurt." Bonnie wasn't the only member of the family who could be persistent.

"I'll talk to my wife about it and get back to you, OK?"

Before the end of the week, Jim called and said that he and his wife would be willing to look things over. "Besides, a couple days out of town might do me some good."

After giving Jim and Sarah a tour of the ranch, I said to Jim, "If God sent Moses into the wilderness for forty years to tend His sheep, might it not be possible that God would love you so much He would send you to Garden Valley for four years to tend to His 'lambs'? We're looking for men of faith to help redirect these kids' lives."

Back home in Washington state, Jim discovered that his friends encouraged him to come to PATCH instead of pursuing the other options he had in mind. Jim accepted our job offer and came to the ranch to be a mentor in the girls' dorm. About the same time a troubled young lady named Angie was placed under our care. She didn't want to be there, and she was determined to get her point across to whomever she met. Before long Angie took out her anger on gentle Jim Smith. She punched him, knocking him to the ground.

Certain he would be discouraged and thinking of leaving, I called Jim into my office. His response to my questions was, "No, I'm not discouraged, and I'm not leaving. I think that while she's been here, Angie has met up with the love of God, and she doesn't know how to handle it."

Jim did so well as a mentor that when an opening came in our counseling department, we offered him the position. To his surprise, his list of counselees included Angie. During one of their counseling sessions Angie became so angry that she threw a chair at his head. He ducked.

Again, worried that he might quit, I asked Jim how he felt.

"I feel wonderful! I believe God's love is getting through to Angie. I wouldn't leave for anything now. And look at all these other young people who deep down inside feel the same way."

In this case, God had worked a miracle for Project PATCH through an unfortunate job loss.

restoring
troubled youth

Project PATCH began simply as a foster-care provider. It has grown into a state-licensed treatment facility, a school with accreditation with Joint Commission on Accreditation of Healthcare Organizations (JAY-CO), and a premier mental-health facility. Operating at first out of a single office, PATCH is now located on a 169-acre ranch on the Payette River. Currently PATCH is branching out into other arenas to provide additional yet compatible services in Goldendale, Washington. And who knows what God has planned next for Project PATCH?

Our entire mission is restoring troubled youth, not only for the present but for future generations to come. Our reason for existing is to help kids change their lives. Yet not all young people make long-term changes while at PATCH. For some, it takes a while before they can pull it all together. Rene was one such young lady.

Constant turmoil followed Rene wherever she went, including to the ranch. Her destructive behavior caused her to be sent out on the wilderness camp more than once. About nine months after she returned home, I received a call from her mother stating that Rene's younger sister was going through similar problems. The mother hastened to explain the reason for her call. "There's probably no need to send Becky to PATCH because Rene has offered to take Becky out on a 'wilderness trek' and teach her skills such as building a shelter, cooking over a campfire, and eating lentils and rice."

* * *

"I hate you! I hate you! I hate you!" Alicia screamed and stomped her feet. "I want out of here! I want out of here now, and you're not going to stop me." A moan of pain from deep within mingled with the fourteen-year-old's hysterical cries. Emotionally spent, she collapsed into the arms of two female staff members. Holding her gently in their arms on the riverbank, they waited for her to speak.

After a few minutes they lowered Alicia to the forest floor and sat down beside her. No one spoke. The sounds of wind whispering through the tall trees, the aroma of pine needles, the sight of dragonflies darting from place to place produced an aura of peace for the runaway and for the two counselors in pursuit.

Providing a safe environment that is consistent and nonthreatening is an essential part of PATCH's therapy program. The women understood the girl's background. Alicia had run, hoping to drown out the hurt her grandfather had regularly inflicted on her since she was six years old. A sexually abusive grandfather, her father in prison for drug possession, her mother dead, the girl was terrified of her future.

Leaning her head against the rough bark of an evergreen, Alicia sighed. "I don't know where to go! I don't have anyone to care for me!"

"We're here for you, Alicia."

"But that's not the same . . ." Her plaintive wail touched the counselors' hearts.

"No, it's not."

"I just want to be a kid again. I wish I could go back to being the little girl I was before my grandfather began . . ." Her voice broke. ". . . doing what he did to me."

"I know." One of the counselors touched the girl's shoulder. "I know."

"Yet I remember what it was like before Mama died and Daddy went to prison. Drunk most of the time, he used to beat us both. I don't want to go back to that!" She squeezed her eyes closed. "Oh, I don't know what I want! I just want the pain to stop! That's what I want!"

It took Alicia two years before she stopped sabotaging her progress at PATCH. One day she was overheard saying, "I am happier when I'm in trouble than when I'm good. I feel safer that way."

Most young people aren't initially happy to be at PATCH. Justin was so unhappy about the prospect that on the way from the airport, he yanked the steering wheel out of his father's hands. The car careened out of control and rolled into the ditch. Justin's attempt at a reprieve from being sent to PATCH was short-lived. When the police arrived on the scene of the accident, they placed the fifteen-year-old in custody until the PATCH staff could come and pick him up.

A couple of months into his stay with us, Justin decided to run from the ranch. The problem was he bolted while Rob, a sixty-year-old staff member, was watching. Rob set chase even though we do not encourage staff members to be heroic. Wrestling a youth to the ground is not in their job description.

As he plowed through the woods, Justin heard something chasing him. Thinking it might be a cougar or a bear, he glanced over his shoulder to see Rob in pursuit. "Go back! Go back!" Justin shouted. "Can't you see I'm running away?"

"I can see that," Rob panted. "I thought I'd just run with you."

Frustrated, Justin tried to outdistance Rob. When both were totally winded, Rob called, "Justin, would you wait a minute so I can catch my breath?"

Justin halted. A puzzled look crossed his face. *Am I hearing right? I'm running away and Rob wants me to wait for him?* In the few months the boy had been at the ranch he had learned to appreciate and respect the staff members in spite of his unresolved personal issues. But this was going too far, asking for a breather when he was running away! Yet Justin waited for Rob to catch up. They chatted for a bit. Rob never once placed his hands on Justin to restrain him. That would be a loss of respect.

With normal breathing restored, he gestured toward Justin. "I'm ready to go if you are."

Incredulous, the fifteen-year-old shrugged and resumed running, with Rob matching him step for step. Again he tried to dissuade Rob from accompanying him. "Go back! Don't you know I'm running away? You're too old to do this!"

Rob nodded and continued running. Some distance later, Rob called again. "Justin, can we rest again? I need to catch my breath."

Though impatient to have to interrupt his adventure toward freedom, Justin reluctantly walked back through the underbrush to where Rob had stopped. No words were exchanged this time. But after a few awkward minutes, Justin sprinted down the trail, leaving Rob behind. It wasn't long before Justin realized that he couldn't hear branches snapping behind him and no panting for breath. He turned around and discovered that Rob wasn't running with him this time. Concerned that Rob might be having a heart attack from all the running, Justin cautiously retraced his steps until he spotted Rob relaxing under a tree.

Justin sat down, and they visited for a few more minutes. From the conversation, Justin could tell Rob really cared about him, yet the boy craved his freedom. Covered with scratches from the underbrush and exhausted from the three sprints through the woods, Rob stood to leave. "You go ahead, Justin, if you must. I'm too old to run with you any farther. What I want you to know, however, is we love you and wish you the best."

Rob started his long journey back toward the ranch. Without a word the fifteen-year-old fell into step beside the exhausted sixty-year-old counselor. Together they began Justin's journey toward healing.

Later as I reviewed Rob's report, I thought of how often I'd run away only to find God matching me step by step. I remembered Jonah's and Elijah's attempts to run from Him and how God loved them so much He didn't give up on them—nor did He take away their right to choose.

* * *

PATCH isn't a lockdown facility, nor do we choose to be intrusive to the point of embarrassment for the kids. As a result, there is always the potential that a child who is determined to run away will, in fact, run.

Teenagers Kathy, Samantha, and Barbara decided to run away one moon-lit night. After stuffing their beds so that it appeared as if they were tucked in and sleeping, they crawled out of an upper-story bedroom window and disappeared into the shadows. Their goal was to hike to Boise and catch a bus for home. Because they knew that if they ran along the side the road, some-one would see them, pick them up, and bring them back to the ranch, they planned to hike over Charter Mountain, which is directly behind the ranch. They would first have to wade across the south fork of the Payette River, and then climb four thousand feet to the top of Charter Mountain, where they hoped to find some trails that would lead them to Boise.

We knew quite soon after their departure that they were gone. We searched along the highway and found no one. That Samantha had severe asthma problems concerned us. We were surprised she'd agree to run away in the first place.

Hiking over rough terrain in the middle of the night is difficult, and it is hard to calculate which direction one is heading. The girls spent all night climbing the mountain and descending to what they thought was the other side. By nine o'clock in the morning, tired, scratched, and hungry, they happened to come out on the road three miles downriver from where they started. They looked like refugees of war. As an act of providence, one of the PATCH staff was hiking along the road looking for any sign of their having passed that way. When he saw them standing on the opposite side of the river, he burst into tears as did the girls. By that time they were no longer anxious to run, nor did they ever attempt to do so again.

Running from the ranch is reasonably safe as there is really nowhere to go, or at least it is a long distance to get there; but when we take the youth on a wilderness survival retreat in the back country, we have to institute safety measures to prevent them from fleeing into the wilds of Idaho. As they prepare for bed, they must surrender their shoes and their outer clothing. This worked for everyone but Ruthie and Kelly, who chose to hitchhike all the way to Boise barefoot, wearing only their PJs and their sleeping bags.

The next morning when the police picked them up in Boise, they fabricated a story about being made to stand out in the wilderness without their shoes and their outer clothing because they'd refused to obey the rules. Their exaggerated story was an effort to solicit enough sympathy to keep them from having to return to PATCH.

The story about the two girls who ran away from Project PATCH hit the evening news on one of the local television stations. As the reporter prepared to air the story, he asked us to explain. He was hoping for a "juicy" story that would make sensational news. We assured him that the girls had not been forced to stand out in the cold minus their clothes and shoes until they agreed to obey our rules. By the time the story aired, the police had made a full investigation and determined that the girls had run because they hadn't wanted to participate in the wilderness program and not because they were being abused. The anticipated sensational story about child abuse dissolved into the reality of two highly rebellious teens. When they were returned to the ranch—which is always the case—they had to return to the same program from which they'd run away.

We learned early on to keep our vehicles locked and the keys secured because the fastest option most runaway kids choose is to steal a car. Robert stole one of our trucks and drove to the Boise airport, where he convinced the airline agent that his wallet had been stolen, and therefore, he didn't have any identification for the flight he wished to take. (This was prior to September 11, 2001.) Before leaving the ranch he had stolen a hundred dollars out of the office—enough for his ticket home.

When he had to change planes at another airport, Robert phoned his mother and told her what he had done and asked her to pick him up at the airport.

"I am not going to pick you up at the airport! You are not coming home." Robert's mother was adamant. "If you show up here, I'll have the police there to take you to jail!"

"But, Mom . . ."

"No 'buts'! You get yourself back to the ranch as fast as you can!"

With his plans in shambles, Robert called the ranch to tell us that he was returning.

Another young man stole a neighbor's vehicle and escaped as far as Ontario, Oregon. When he called his mother, she then called PATCH.

Together they decided that the best thing the boy could do was to return to Idaho before he was arrested for interstate transportation of a stolen vehicle. The police picked him up at a rest area and brought him back to the ranch and returned the car to its rightful owner.

With the exception of one, all of these young people became PATCH success stories. Running away is not a serious issue among the kids at PATCH, but occasionally it does happen. Without exception, all the runaways had a history of running prior to coming to the ranch, and without exception they quit running. As one young man put it, "I finally realized I couldn't run anywhere that was going to be safer or more caring than PATCH. I just had to get over a very bad and dangerous habit."

* * *

Sixteen-year-old Jamie couldn't believe her eyes. Although she had made a lot of bad choices in her life, she concluded that this was the worst one she'd ever made. Her parents had packed up her belongings and had "someone" take her on a "little trip." Exhausted, she'd immediately fallen asleep when she climbed into the car. When she awoke four hours later, she found herself at the Project PATCH ranch.

Jaime had become a danger to herself: late-night parties, boyfriends, high-speed "chicken" races on darkened streets, and barreling through stop signs and traffic lights. Her parents were terrified she would destroy herself.

The girl tried to run away, but since she'd been asleep for the entire journey, she had no idea where she was. The first time Jaime tried to run, she hiked a trail that circled around and brought her right back to the PATCH buildings. Then something happened that changed her life. This is her story as she tells it:

"My life was a mess. Plain and simple! I was extremely into drugs, sex, alcohol, and gangs. I was also living on the streets or with people I'd randomly meet downtown. Basically I thought life was one big party. I thought I couldn't die, well, not anytime soon anyway. I felt invincible; after all I have been through, I had never been seriously injured and obviously not killed. Finally, my family decided that I was either going to end up pregnant, with AIDS, or dead. So on one of the rare times I was home, they had someone take me away to Garden Valley, Idaho, to be a resident of PATCH.

"I also had made myself numb to any emotional pain for that matter. I just couldn't feel. After living on the streets with my 'brothers,' in gangs, I saw things that should have horrified me, but they didn't. I remember a time watching my brothers beat the living daylights out of someone over drugs, and I actually laughed. I was twisted. I just didn't care. Why allow myself to feel? I had too much other crud to deal with [like] where was I going to sleep? What was I gonna eat? Was this guy I was going home with going to hurt me? These were all questions I asked myself on more than one occasion.

"I dropped out of school in the beginning of my sophomore year; I barely went my freshman year. So I didn't do anything all day except be with my boyfriend at the time and get high. I was constantly hurting myself and letting others do the same thing. Use and abuse!

"I tried to run away from my problems by putting up a huge front of sex, drugs, and alcohol. I acted like everything was fine, but on the inside I was in a rage. I hated my life; I hated feeling so used up. I tried running away from PATCH, three days after I got there, in the end of January! Obviously it didn't work. Anything that was even remotely hard, I ran away from. Someone who cared for me, I ran away from love . . . yes, I even ran away from that.

"Looking back now I am amazed. I have memories of things that hurt me, but I know I am stronger because of the things I went through. And, after being at PATCH for almost seven months, my negative behaviors are starting to change. But they just started changing drastically this last month. I can feel again! I have cried so many more tears, but I have also laughed, I mean really laughed! Yes, the pain is real, but so is the joy!"

As Jaime put the beginning of her new life into perspective, she said, "I can't believe the changes that are happening to me. My callousness and indifference to life all came on so gradually I didn't realize I was such a mess. But now I can see clearly what a dangerous position I was in. I was so close to death. I thank God for PATCH and the chance God gave me to feel again, to love again, and most important, to have a conscience again."

* * *

"Many, O Lᴏʀᴅ my God, are the wonders you have done. The things You planned for us no one can recount to you; were I to speak and tell of them, they would be too many to declare" (Psalm 40:5, NIV).

Only the awesome God, Jehovah, the "ever revealing One," could do all He has done for His hurting children. Through Project PATCH, I've learned so much about myself, about the love Bonnie and I share, about my fabulous son and daughter, and about the myriad of caring and willing people whom God has placed in just the right place at just the right time to fulfill our needs.

Over the years, Jehovah-Jireh, "the Lord our Provider," never has chosen to give us more than we need in any given situation. Time and again I have been forced to my knees to admit that caring for these precious children is His job, not mine. He is in control. And every trial reminds me that, as much as He loves me and desires to meet the needs of Project PATCH, He is also busy perfecting my character.

The abused little boy who grew up craving his biological father's love and always being rejected has had the opportunity to learn over and over again that his Eternal Father loves him so much more than he ever could imagine. That perfect Father does provide, just as He promises in His Word.

And, in turn, I have been privileged to pass on that lesson to hundreds of hurting, troubled youth who have no hope for the future and have never experienced a Father's genuine, unconditional love. I thank God for being willing to use a person such as me. My life has proved the saying that God doesn't call the qualified; rather, He qualifies the called.

And what lies ahead for Project PATCH? For me and for my family?

I can only imagine and say with the apostle Paul in Romans 8, as paraphrased in *The Message* Bible, "This resurrection life [I] received from God is not a timid, grave-tending life. It's adventurously expectant, greeting God with a childlike 'What's next, Papa?' "

If you enjoyed this book, you'll enjoy these also:

If Parenting Is a Three-Ring Circus, How Come I'm Not the Ringmaster?
Tom Sanford. You've read *Wounded Healer.* You know about the wisdom, experience, and good humor that characterize the life and work of Tom Sanford. In this appealing book on parenting, Tom has distilled his hard-won knowledge about creative ways to raise great kids into twelve succinct, easy-to-read chapters. When it comes to dealing with your children, Tom says "Logic is never the point. Love is. Forgiveness is. Valuing another person is."
0-936785-97-7. Paperback.
US$12.99, Can$17.99

Battered to Blessed: My Personal Journey
Brenda Walsh with Kay D. Rizzo. To look at "Miss Brenda" today singing gospel music or hosting her children's TV program on 3ABN, you'd never know the horrors of domestic violence that she once endured. ***Battered to Blessed*** is Brenda Walsh's amazing journey from pain to peace, and to loving again, trusting again, and living a whole new life of incredible joy in Jesus!
0-8163-2067-5. Paperback.
US$14.99, Can$22.49.

Chosen
Ron and Nancy Rockey. ***Chosen*** is the true story of a boy who wasn't wanted by his family. Rejected and feeling unworthy of love or affection, Ron Rockey grew up full of anger and hate. That anger landed Ron in prison several times before his life began to change. It was a slow, gradual change, and in this self-disclosing story, he walks you through step by painful step as he runs, falls, and gets back up, only to fall again and again. But God didn't give up on Ron.
0-8163-1900-6. Paperback.
US$12.99, Can$17.99.

Order from your ABC by calling **1-800-765-6955**, or get online and shop our virtual store at **www.AdventistBookCenter.com**.
• Read a chapter from your favorite book
• Order online
• Sign up for email notices on new products

Prices subject to change without notice.